The Golden Retriever Companion

A Chronicle of Joy

Catherine O'Driscoll

Acknowledgments

There are so many people who have helped in the preparation of this book. My thanks go out to everyone whose name appears within these pages.

To be as comprehensive as possible, I contacted many dog magazines, medical and country pursuit publications, breeders and showers, Golden Retriever clubs, authorities, charities and organisations to invite stories about Golden Retrievers. Apologies if the kennel or organisation you believe should be included, has not been included – although it is not my intention to produce a book that comprehensively charts the history of the breed.

It is thanks to all who have warmed to the idea of a tribute to the *personalities* of Golden Retrievers that this book has been made possible. I have discovered that those who are owned by Golden Retrievers are enormously busy people, so their help is all the more appreciated.

Miss Joan Gill and Mrs Daphne Philpott of the famous Westley and Standerwick kennels have very kindly and graciously read the completed manuscript to ensure that I have not passed on inaccurate information. Their extensive knowledge and love of the breed is already committed to legend. They have worked in partnership with Mr Mervyn Philpott for many, many years to produce outstanding dogs. They have made a life-giving and lasting contribution not only to the Golden Retriever breed, but also to the lives of thousands of human beings around the world.

I would like to thank Mike and Jackie Grubb for their kindness and considerable efforts in providing information about Goldens in the United States. My admiration goes to them for the love and care they show towards their canine friends, and I thank them for the invaluable support they have given me in the preparation of this book.

Ed and Marallyn Wight of the USA have provided all the essential background for the preparation of the tracking section. I have had the expert help of two highly experienced vets, Mrs Ann Hayes MRCVS BVSc of Northamptonshire, now retired, and Mr Cliff Alderman, spokesman of the Small Animals Veterinary Association and a practising vet in Oxford. In addition, the Yankee Golden Retriever Rescue has shared important tips about poisons and general practical health matters. Animal behaviourist Erica Peachey has given extensive help in the obedience chapter; John Seymour and Roy and Pat Bartlett have generously contributed to the breeding section; and Dorothy Cyster has offered much needed moral support and extensive experience in the preparation of the bereavement chapter.

Thanks go also to the first Lord Tweedmouth who, between 1868 and 1889, created Golden Retrievers; to the ultimate Creator; and to the conscientious breeders who remain true to the temperament and physical beauty of the breed.

This book has been particularly enhanced by the many photographs which have winged their way here from Golden Retriever owners around the world. Thank you to everyone who trusted their treasured photographs to us, and to the many respected professional photographers, including Sally Anne Thompson, Philip Tull, Val Connolly, and Juliann Houseman Caruthers. Special thanks go to Susan Rezy who has worked with me from the beginning, and who kept amazing me with her talents and more and more beautiful photographs.

Thanks to James Tweed in the design of the book. Connie Gray has been an angel, as has Margaret Copley, and every single person mentioned within these pages.

Finally, my thanks go in great measure to my husband John who has donated many of his photographs and a great deal of his time to produce the finished manuscript and, most important of all, encouraged and supported me in my work. John loves Golden Retrievers as much as I do: together we have shared our lives with some remarkable personalities.

This book is as much a tribute to the people who have kept the wonderful temperament in the breed as it is to the dogs themselves. Do let me know if you have stories to tell. You never know, there may be a sequel!

Oliver

Dedication

On Monday, 2nd September 1991, the best friend I have ever had died. Oliver had packed several lifetimes of fun and jollity into four short years, bringing my husband John and I such an abundance of happiness that his loss, which came quite suddenly and unpredictably, was devastating.

Oliver was a handsome huggable Golden Retriever, a positive delight to have around. Oliver was a real comedian who made us roar with laughter: out loud, every day of his life. He was funny and wise, totally irrepressible, and he had more energy and enthusiasm for life than any human being I know. When he wanted to play – which was most of the time – Oliver would leap upon someone, grab their arm gently but firmly in his mouth, and pull them into the garden.

Oliver Twist couldn't have picked a pocket more surreptitiously than our Oliver. Pockets with zips, tight fitting jeans – nothing could prevent him from obtaining that handkerchief or bunch of keys. Handbags and shoes were part of the act, too, and our guests soon learnt to be tidy with Oliver around. He was a Retriever in every sense of the word.

His very big, very black, nose was into everything, and everything was a big adventure. Bags, cupboards, linen baskets... nothing was safe. Even the plumbers and electricians who came to the house from time to time had to keep their tools, nuts and bolts, very tightly under control. He collected items as intently as he did people and other dogs. He was ready to be friends with everyone, and few could resist his good natured advances.

We learnt a lot from Oliver: how to be happy from a true master of the art, how to value every moment, how to take pleasure in little things, and how it is to be totally and unconditionally loved.

Throughout the world, there are thousands of 'Olivers' who give an abundance of love and happiness to human beings. People who are lonely; people who are disabled; people who need a job of work doing; and people who need a reliable, trustworthy friend in an increasingly hostile world.

This book is dedicated to Oliver, the dog who scattered rays of Golden happiness to anyone who would play, and to the people who have shared a lifetime of companionship with this truly remarkable breed: the Golden Retriever.

Limited First Edition - 1994

Written by Catherine O'Driscoll

Book design by James Tweed

Published by Abbeywood Publishing

 (a division of Abbeywood Investments Ltd)

Printed in Portugal

ISBN 0 9523048 0 5

Table of Contents

A Unique Brand of Joy

Goldens love children

This book was born when Oliver died. It is my tribute to Golden Retrievers and, extending the theme, to all dogs and animals who bring their own unique brand of joy to Creation.

As many dog owners know, there has been much negative thought surrounding the whole subject of dog ownership. People who do not own dogs object, quite understandably, to the waste products of animals in public places. As a consequence, dogs are currently banned from the towns and cities of fifteen countries. The newspapers are generally brimming with stories about dirty dogs, nuisance dogs and noisy dogs. Plans to ban dogs from common parkland, beaches and other areas abound.

Shortly after Oliver died, I received a letter from the local parish council threatening to ban our dogs from the playing field. My initial reaction was one of anger, and I responded with extreme hostility. How dare they ban living creatures? Where were we expected to walk? We were not welcomed on farmland, and we didn't want to dodge traffic on the roads. There seemed to be no place for us. My mind conjured up images of me, and my dogs, walking to the park with large placards to defy their injunction. My darling Oliver had died, and my heart was broken, and it seemed they wanted to be rid of us all.

But, just as hate cannot be dissolved by its mirror image, opposition is not weakened by counter opposition. Peace comes from love – something Golden Retrievers know a lot about.

And so I reformed. I now scoop all the poops – not just our dogs' but all the poops in the park, using a sort of dustpan on a stick which means the task is not unpleasant in the least. Some people will say that I am taking matters to extremes – but this was the only way I could find to turn negativity about dogs into enjoyment of dogs in the place where I live. Now all my neighbours and their dogs are free to enjoy this beautiful setting, and the complaints have been eliminated.

But there was another matter to attend to. I wanted people to understand that dogs do a great deal to enrich society, and the lives of human beings. Our house, for example, is always brimming with our neighbours' children, children who adore animals. We are happy to stop in the street and talk with all sorts of people, people who adore animals. And many new friends tell me how much they enjoy watching our Golden Retrievers as they play in the park.

Life is like playing the piano: the more you practice, the better you get. Love is the same, and loving animals provides the perfect practice before going on to encompass all of creation.

2

The joys and tribulations of being owned by a Golden

Golden Retrievers are sunny creatures who bring love and companionship to all who would ask. They love life and help others to love life. They are happy characters who make others happy. They uplift the human spirit. Within these pages you will learn how to care for another living creature, and you will discover that the vast majority of dogs, illustrated most beautifully by the Golden Retriever, have a place on this earth: a valuable, important and life-giving place.

We have four Golden Retrievers, the limit having been set by the number of feet and hands one person has available at any one time with which to stroke and caress this affectionate breed.

People have often asked me how I cope with four large dogs. My answer is simple: I want to. I cannot imagine life without them, they have enriched it so greatly. You will find many people like me within these pages: people who just wouldn't be without their Golden friends.

Being incapable of judging objectively, I asked animal behaviour consultant Erica Peachey whether she thought Golden Retrievers were in any way different to other dogs. Erica concluded that it is the owners who are different. They seem so happy, so friendly, she told me. Neither of us could decide which came first: the happy owner, or the happy dog.

It is true that Golden Retrievers carry perpetual smiles. You can even see their distinct laugh, and many of them have a most unusual way of speaking: a small indignant woof, pricked ears and alert eyes mean it's time to play; 'grrrerrerr mm grrerrerr' means 'where have you been, I've been fed up waiting for you'; and a ferocious, deep, belly-rumbling bark generally means no more than 'let's play tuggie'.

Whilst we can teach our Goldens a great deal, I believe that Golden Retrievers can, in turn, teach the human race many valuable lessons. I am always confused when human beings talk about the superiority of the human species over animals – for my Goldens seem to live the kind of life, and exhibit the sort of integrity, that mankind mistakenly believes is unique to the human species. I would even go so far as to say that Golden Retrievers provide a perfect model for the human race: if we could be so slow to judge one-another; if we could be so willing to be friends.

I have learnt, through watching, to trust my Goldens in the company of children and frail adults. Sometimes, I have to make sure that the children aren't harming the dogs because no-one has yet taught them how to respect living creatures, and the Goldens are too well mannered to respond.

4

Sophie and Samson

3

Samson

My four Retrievers – Chappie, Sophie, Prudence and Samson – fill me with awe, and constantly earn my respect. Big gentle Chappie, who licks Pru dry when she's been out swimming, and allowed the rascal puppy, Samson, to plunge his sharp little teeth into his neck. When our darling Oliver died, Chappie took to sitting next to his grave, so much did this 'dumb animal' miss his friend.

Soft and gentle Sophie appeals to my better nature when I raise my voice, and mischievously steals my handkerchief when a sad film makes me cry. Late at night, when the rest of the house is asleep, Sophie and I have our time together. She sits across the room and talks to me from her soft and comfortable chair, and I must go to her to whisper sweet words in her ears.

And bossy Prudence, the protector, who would put herself in between Chappie and Oliver if their game got out of hand. When we took Samson out for his first walk, it was Prudence who flung herself as a protective barrier between the little puppy and a neighbour's adult dog; and Prudence who snarled and barked at the strange man one day who, I am sure, would otherwise have attacked me. More recently, while Chappie has been recovering from an illness, it is Prudence who deflects the exuberant Samson away from Chaps, protecting our oldest Golden from the youthful two-year-old.

A family Christmas by the fire

5

Smile

6

"Bear & TD" (Camerons Quarterback)

7

Pinecrests Linebacker TD (Bear) and Camerons Quarterback (TD)

Their inherent goodness was most evident while Samson learnt what was, and what was not, acceptable Golden behaviour. When Samson flew at them with his needle sharp teeth, Chappie, Sophie and Pru reacted with extreme gentility. When I shouted a loud 'No!' to stop Samson misbehaving, Sophie would look up and beg me with her eyes, and by waving her paw, not to be too harsh.

And Prudence took on the role of mother, intently cleaning his ears and his eyes, gently mouthing him in mock fights, and playing 'you're not getting the ball off me' to keep him occupied.

Goldens are well known for their vivacious personalities, and for their gentility and sensitivity. It is these characteristics which make them so perfect as guide dogs, PAT (Pets As Therapy) Dogs, and assistance dogs. It is often said that they make the ideal family pet, for they truly adore children and show a remarkable kindness and understanding towards the elderly and infirm.

Equally, they can make superb sporting and working dogs. They are never happier than when up to their necks in water retrieving a bird, or running through the fields and woods, using their powerful bodies and their alert minds to the full.

The breed's intelligence makes them easy to train, but I have found that this intelligence can be a two-edged sword – for it is not a breed for anyone who needs a passive pet.

Contrary to popular opinion, a Golden Retriever is not a 'background' dog, the 'musak' of the canine world. I say this because the Golden Retriever is an incredibly popular breed; people think they are easier to own than many other breeds you can choose.

Yet, every year around the world, hundreds of Golden Retrievers get 'sent back to the shop' or dumped on the street. Dog ownership is a two-way relationship, and it is sometimes easy to under-estimate the time that must be devoted to keep that pet both mentally and physically healthy.

To some, the joys of being owned by a Golden are endless. Those of us who are confirmed 'Goldies' positively thrive upon the responsibilities that our beloveds place upon us. We are the ones who place our footsteps in the virgin white snow when everyone else is home by the fire; we are the ones who trudge through the rain, sniffing the damp earth and the rotting twigs, with tiny pearls of water dripping from our noses – while most Poodles and Yorkshire Terriers remain indoors, snug and warm.

If you want the sort of dog who will always sit quietly in the corner, then don't get a Golden. If you want a dog that doesn't interrupt in the middle of a conversation, don't get a Golden. If you have a hectic social life and you want to keep it, then don't get a Golden. If you covet your possessions and don't want them to be retrieved, can't stand dog hairs, don't like rain, can't walk far, and haven't got a sense of humour, then take warning, because these are all intrinsic elements of being owned by a Golden Retriever.

If, on the other hand, you want a friend to join the family and become a central part of it, you couldn't make a better choice. Golden Retrievers like nothing better than to be at the centre of it all, pleasing the ones they love (and they tend to love everyone); they are immensely funny and love to see you laugh; and they are sensitive and kind. In the right hands, a Golden Retriever responds well to training and becomes a positive asset to have around.

Unlike children, Goldens never want a new bike – but they will need almost as much of your attention as that naughty human toddler. Unlike more passive pets like hamsters, Goldens sleep at night (usually) but don't expect your best friend to sleep all day, too. He'll want plenty of exercise, both mental and physical.

Be prepared for the tribulations as well as the joys: the laughter and the tears. There will be trips to the vet, and times of worry – and he won't be able to tell you what's wrong; there will be his funny little habits to make you laugh, but there will also be stolen slippers and finding someone to care for him when the family goes abroad. Finally, there will be the unbearable loss when your Golden finally dies, and the heartbreak that this entails.

When you bring your new puppy home, be prepared for him to turn your house inside out. This is one little creature who needs time to learn, and his natural instincts in the meantime won't show much respect for your settled routine, your furniture, or your sleep pattern. You will need to get yourself organised in advance, try to understand his needs, and blame yourself – not the puppy – if he has failed to comply immediately with your wishes. It is up to you to make sure that the carpet isn't chewed and the house training is effected without mishap – see the training and puppy chapters rather than losing your temper!

It is the wise person who recognises the impact any dog will have on the household. If you have time to spare, a good garden or open fields nearby, sufficient funds, and a true love of animals, then get that Golden Retriever. He's waiting for you with open paws, to share his irresistible golden personality.

Chappie

9

Chappie loves Cars

10

Samson loves Chappie

11

Chappie was our first Golden Retriever, a rescue dog, the product of a broken home who came to us when he was 18 months old. I had waited years for him because I worked and couldn't bear the thought of saying goodbye to a dog every morning, leaving him to endless days of solitary confinement. Now that I was working from home I had my chance – and I took it.

On the plus side, a rescue dog usually comes fully house-trained – and Chappie arrived the perfect gentleman. He had been taught not to jump up on the furniture. He wouldn't eat his food until he was given permission. He stayed downstairs, and wouldn't come up unless invited. He didn't even bark.

We had been warned that Chappie was extremely boisterous. Could we cope? We had answered 'great', because we welcomed the thought of a dog with a real personality. When he arrived at our house, though, Chappie had a good sniff around to get his bearings and promptly lay down to sleep.

We waited for weeks for the boisterous side of Chappie to come out – yet he was a picture of calm and tranquillity. Boisterous? Chappie? We couldn't work it out. In fact, Chappie was calm to the point of lugubriousity. 'Chappie, be boisterous,' John would urge. We had to encourage and entice him to play, and there was a look of abject horror on his face if he accidentally mouthed one of us in his enthusiasm.

Our hearts truly went out to Chappie. He was a sad sorry creature who seemed to have been disciplined to the point where his spirit was almost broken. We had to teach him that he was allowed to play, that he wouldn't be told off.

Chappie went through the manual at the veterinary surgery: one illness followed by another – kennel cough, a hypothyroid gland, leg strains, 'hot spots', ear infections – you name it and Chappie got it. I even began to worry lest the vet thought I fancied him! It was a new surgery, and I think Chappie's fees practically got the practice going.

And yet the pluses far outweighed the problems. The look of joy on his face the first time he was allowed into the bedroom. The pretty prancing, like a frisky pony, when told it was walkie time. The concern he showed when one of us was ill, and the comfortable companionship he gave beside the fire on cold winter evenings.

Yet still, I couldn't understand why Chappie had been labelled as boisterous. And then one day, several years later, the picture became clearer when a new wooden shed arrived. After it had been erected in the garden, the dogs (by now there were four) went inside to inspect, and came out again quite satisfied. Chappie, on the other hand, took himself inside and stood up on his hind legs howling dolefully through the window. The door was open, and yet Chappie acted as though he were a prisoner.

Chappie

Chappie, you will remember, came from a broken home. Could it be that he had spent his days locked up in the shed until someone arrived to let him out? We will never really know, but it explains to me why Chappie's previous owners might have described him as boisterous. Which intelligent person would react differently in the same circumstances?

Chappie is so intelligent that I sometimes have trouble thinking of him as a dog. He doesn't, for example, always do as he is told because, being intelligent, he has often thought of a better course of action all by himself. Imagine, then, how you might feel if you were shut up in a confined space day after day, and tell me how you would react.

Would you run and deliriously hug every nice person who comes to see you and relieve you from the monotony of your own company; would you hurl all your words out in one great breath; would you even go a little mad, become a little too hot to handle? I wouldn't blame you if you did.

I have seen Chappie's personality change so often as our own circumstances have changed, that I really don't believe that a complex creature like a Golden Retriever can be categorised as good or bad, boisterous or placid.

When we have moved home; had elderly relatives to stay; gone walking with a friend who is blind; had children round to play;

introduced new puppies – Chappie's personality has changed to accommodate the new circumstances. He can be gentle, playful, thoughtful, boisterous, mellow – everything. Like the true gentleman, Chappie adapts.

Chappie is proof positive that dogs can speak: one look for 'I want to play', another look for 'isn't it walkie time?', and another which means 'can I have some fresh water in my bowl please?'. And not only can Chappie speak, he also has a keen sense of responsibility.

For example, when Prudence accidentally jumped over the garden wall in her enthusiasm to tell a passing hedgehog exactly what she thought of it, Chappie came straight into the house to tell me what had happened. His eyes said it all, and I went outside to investigate and rescue her.

Whilst Chappie came to us with perfect manners in the home, we had our work cut out in the fields and in the woods. Here, he was a hooligan of the first degree, totally ruled by his nose which could lead him practically anywhere. Whoosh, there's a fox, zoom, there's a rabbit, and frantic digging if there's a mole about. Then Chappie would be lost to the world, oblivious to calls and totally absorbed by the source of the smell.

Goldens are outdoor dogs

For the first few years we lost Chappie over and over again. One memorable loss occurred when I had a horrible dose of flu and it was pouring with rain. John was away – and Golden Retrievers need their morning walk whether you like it or not! Chappie disappeared, and I ended up trudging through the fields for hours searching for him. Eventually I took my thoroughly soaked, bedraggled and frustrated self home to call the police station . . . only to discover that Chappie had been sitting happily in front of a fire in a compassionate neighbour's house eating Pedigree Chum. (I told you he was intelligent.)

There are two possible reasons for Chappie's propensity to run off. It may be that this is a characteristic of some strains of the breed, and I have certainly heard of other Goldens with this personality trait. A second reason might be that Chappie was never taught, as a puppy, that it was a good thing to have a good run, but also good to come back when called. Once the pattern has been set as a puppy, it is sometimes difficult to change it.

Some people would have kept Chappie on the lead, but I couldn't bear the thought of keeping a dog, who had been bred for working, imprisoned in this way. Goldens live for their walks; one of their greatest enjoyments is running unhampered through the fields, so it was up to us to work on him, and let him know that if he stayed close he wouldn't be dragged off home or locked on the lead.

Today, we have almost conquered the problem – but there is still a point which, if crossed, represents the point of no return and Chappie is off.

12

Prudence

Sophie Two Shoes

Our second Retriever, Sophie, came to us when she was four months old and virtually house trained. Sophie was Chappie's present, because we knew that Goldens are gregarious creatures whose primary aim in life is to have friends and companions. We found that it was no real hardship washing two sets of paws after a muddy walk and, apart from vet bills, we didn't find it a great deal more expensive to have two.

Chappie's reaction to his new girlfriend was nothing short of ecstatic, and in no time at all they were charging around the house together and playing tricks on one-another. Their favourite pastime soon became an intense competition, much like human arm-wrestling, which entails seeing who can open their mouth the widest!

I'm absolutely certain that Sophie is a reincarnation of both Marilyn Monroe and Queen Victoria. She is so delicate and proper (and often not amused), yet she's also a naughty blonde with a wiggly bottom and a great sense of fun.

Sophie likes nothing better than to steal something she's not allowed to have: socks, shoes, ties, spectacles (especially if someone is wearing them), and when she does, she scrunches her eyes up and forms her mouth into a broad happy grin. Sophie is a streamline Golden, almost as fast as a Collie, and when she delicately places her paws on the chair and moves up extremely slowly to take the glasses from your face, you hardly know she has touched you. We call her Sophie Two Shoes because one shoe is never enough.

Watching Sophie and Chappie play together proved to be the best entertainment we could have – much more interesting than television. They kept each other fit and happy, and we found that the 'work' involved in Golden ownership halved rather than doubled.

Chappie and Sophie proved the Golden Rule: Goldens are very collectible items, so it wasn't long before we decided to get ourselves a third – but fate decreed we should come home with number four as well.

The Prollies Arrive

We called our two new additions 'The Prollies' (PRu and OLLIE). Prudence had already chosen us on our previous visit by sitting her pretty little self in front of John and barking in the most irresistible manner (I have to say she's not shut up since, but everyone agrees she's still irresistible).

On the next visit, when we went to collect Pru, a small and endearing bundle of Golden fun took hold of my fingers between his teeth and refused to let go. His little tail, and his entire bottom wiggled with joy. It was Oliver.

"We've got to have him," John said. "What, instead of Pru?" I asked. "No, as well as." I can't help thinking that Oliver chose us on that day.

Sophie - Cool Krystal (Abnalls Jolly Roger ex Bia Kandeese)

14

Oliver - Tiarpica Pippin (Abnalls Jolly Roger ex Pride of Westwood)

15

Prudence

What can I tell you about Oliver? Oliver was a joyous creature. He possessed charm in such great measure that, had he wanted to, he could have got away with virtually anything. But he never wanted to. His obedience extended to my thoughts: my wish was his desire. Occasionally in life we come across people and animals who seem to emanate from the sun, and Ollie was one of these.

We used to call him the Mountain Heffalump, because Oliver strode everywhere with great purpose. When out on walks he would find himself the biggest, heaviest log, and with great pride he would saunter along with his gay tail right up in the air. No-one seemed to be able to pass without laughing – you could virtually see the sparks of light and happiness ricocheting off him.

When we went on holiday and stayed in hotels, it was always Oliver who took himself off to say hello to all the other guests. We would call him back, fearing that his presence might not be welcomed – but it always was. He would put his great big paw on someone's lap, and then he would lie down and demand to have his tummy rubbed. If anyone dared stop, he would use his paw as a hook and make them start again. Soon, instead of separate groups of people keeping themselves to themselves, the hotel was one large family, with Oliver at the centre.

Soon after he died, John and I saw a television programme about a native American woman called Twylah Nitsch. Normally the dogs ignore humans on the television, but they all went up and sniffed the screen when Twylah came on. Twylah said this: each being comes into life with a mission and when they fulfil that mission, they return to the Great Mystery. It made sense to me, for Oliver had been the perfect dog, friend, and companion. We had been blessed with his presence for four short years: we had discovered real joy.

As Edgar Bawtree wrote on the death of Benji, "Mission Completed." And we must let go with gratitude.

When Oliver died, we had to find someone to fill the chasm, the gigantic and 'once in a lifetime' presence that he left behind. Samson had a hard act to follow, but he is acquitting himself with vigour.

Samson

At five months of age, little Samson began to change from enjoyable hard work to a considerable pleasure to have around. A puppy is a puppy for such a short space of time, that you have to overlook the frayed carpets, chewed shoes and sleepless nights, and revel in the joy that a puppy brings to any welcoming household.

(Connie Gray made me laugh when she told me the name of her new puppy: "NoJayne." All puppy owners will understand the joke!)

Samson, like all dogs, has a great sense of order: but his seems to be more pronounced. He likes each day to follow a predictable routine and gets upset when we are not doing what we are supposed to be doing at the allotted time. He has now earned himself the title of, "Keeper of the Clock."

It took me longer than usual to complete my household chores one evening when he was five months old, so little Samson grabbed hold of my arm, led me into the TV room, and made me sit down. What a considerate little chap! Samson thinks his real name is "You Again"; he loves me so much he wants to merge with me (starting with his big black nose sinking through my face).

Samson - Blakesley Boyd (Sh. Ch. Sinnheim Sebastian ex Nortonwood Coralie)

Prudence

To anyone who has never had a relationship with a dog, a dog is a fluffy thing with four legs and a tail who disgraces himself in public. And yet, everyone I have spoken with about Golden Retrievers say that they are really PEOPLE in different bodies.

Prudence reminds me of a little girl I knew at school, the little girl we all knew at school with pigtails and freckles: the leader of the gang. Prudence exhibits a strange mixture of personality traits, occasionally found in Goldens, that appears to be tough and ferocious on the outside but is in reality very soft and approachable.

If you didn't know Prudence you certainly wouldn't mess with her: she can sound just like the Hound of the Baskervilles, especially when a cat or a dog appears in the lane by our house, or on the television. In fact, we have great difficulty in watching Crufts on the TV – because Prudence is always in front of it, blocking the view and issuing death threats.

(Our courageous Pru also barks at horses when she's inside the car – but when she's outside of it, and consequently liable to suffer the reprisals, Prudence keeps her mouth shut!)

Pru also has a great line in chat. "Nyom, nyom, nyom," is her favourite saying which, roughly translated means: "I've got a ball in my mouth, isn't it wonderful?" There is pure joy for living in that sound.

Despite her ferocious and noisy comments, Prudence is the lap dog par excellence, the softest cuddliest person you could ever meet. It is Prudence who looks after her brothers and sister, licking them clean; Prudence who goes soft and gooey when there's a baby around; and Prudence who welcomes visitors with big wet kisses. And the children who come to visit always go to Pru for an abundance of love and cuddles.

17

Prudence - (Tiarpica Prudent Miss - litter sister to Oliver)

Golden Retrievers certainly make their presence felt

When you invite a Golden Retriever into your home, you are more or less welcoming the equivalent of an 18-month old child. There are differences, of course, the chief ones being that a Golden doesn't keep asking 'why?', he doesn't take so long to toilet train, and he runs faster than you can!

Be aware that a Golden Retriever comes into the world as a puppy, and many of them leave the world as puppies. Oliver, at the age of four, retained nearly all of the characteristics displayed by Samson at the age of fifteen weeks. Chappie, aged seven, suddenly became a puppy again, charging about the house with Samson, teaching him all the naughty tricks he could remember or invent.

When a Golden Retriever tumbles through your door, you will never again justifiably complain that life is boring.

Some people say that animals don't have personalities – but I can't agree (she said, stomping her foot with resolve). A person, after all, is a unique entity, distinguished from other people by his or her body, ego and mind-set. If you take the time to get to know any animal, you will find that each does have its own unique personality.

Of course, Golden Retrievers do share similar personality *traits* but, again, if you take the time to get to know a number of Golden Retrievers, you will find that each has its own way of seeing and dealing with the world, just as humans do.

I have witnessed dogs show love, affection, jealousy, sympathy, aggression, humour. I have seen dogs perform acts of selfless devotion. I have felt the space between our minds disappear so that we have had the same mind. I have shared understanding with a dog: tangible, positive, certain understanding.

"Ah but you're anthropomorphosising," some will say (just before they throw the steak under the grill). But maybe it is simply convenient to believe that animals are not people in their own rights. Lumped together as a group without individuality, without feelings, aren't they easier to disregard and mistreat? As with all prejudices, doesn't this mean that, because they are not 'one of us', they don't deserve our respect?

In a major feature published by 'New Scientist' in October 1993, it was reported that people with pets tend to have a more positive and humane attitude to animals, the environment, and a tendency to greater 'emotional empathy' for people too. This supports my own belief that, far from running from human company to the non-judgmental company of animals, pet owners are merely extending the circle of love.

'New Scientist' further states that pet owners value their pets as "distinctive personalities with whom they have affectionate relationships." Other research, not covered within this journal, indicates that many of those found guilty of cruelty or violence towards humans, first sharpened their skills on animals.

Research in 'New Scientist' claims that pets are good for your health. Many researchers suspect that this has something to do with the subtle links between mental and physical wellbeing. James Serpell, now at the University of Pennsylvania, argues that it is in friendship that we find the real explanation for pets' beneficial effects on our health.

Studies show that people who feel isolated and depressed are more likely to succumb to illness than people who claim to be contented. Researchers at the University of Cambridge discovered that months after acquiring a cat or a dog, some Britons suffer less from problems such as headache, backache and flu.

Erica Friedmann, now at the City University of New York, found that people who had heart attacks and were socially isolated, were less likely to recover than those who had pets. Warwick Anderson of the Baker Medical Research Institute in Australia, found that the average cholesterol level of patients who owned pets was two per cent lower than those who did not, reducing the risk of heart attack by four per cent.

'New Scientist' also states:

Those with dogs are more likely to experience positive encounters with other people, including prolonged conversations with people who are alone or with children.

Wellbeing doesn't depend on stroking or talking to a pet. Tests indicate that adults and children are more relaxed simply in the presence of a friendly dog.

Pet/human relationships resemble those which psychotherapists try to build. The fact that pets listen and seem to understand, but do not question or evaluate, may be one of their most endearing assets as companions.

And so it is that I choose to consider animals as people in their own right. My Golden Retrievers make me feel so good, that I am honoured to count them amongst my friends, and endeavour to be as good a friend to them, and to other people.

Many who share their homes with Golden Retrievers testify that their lives have been enriched by these gentle, intelligent, creatures with a distinct sense of humour. Interestingly, many people have told me of the friendships that have been developed between individual dogs.

Margaret Copley, who has kept dogs in Norfolk for many years, described the friendship which grew up between her Golden Retriever Sasha and a beautiful black Cocker Spaniel called Chloe: "Sasha and Chloe lived together for quite a while, until the work commitments of my friend forced her to let Chloe go," she said.

"Well it was very strange, because every time I was out with Sasha and she saw a black Cocker Spaniel we had to go and say hello. My cousin, who had taken Chloe, told me that Chloe did the same when there was a Golden Retriever about. Sasha and I called on my cousin one day, and the two girls were so very happy to see each other. They went off for a walk and a swim together and came back wringing wet.

"People don't understand dogs at all. They're just like us. They have friendships, enemies, everything. I do feel that Sasha and Chloe will never forget one-another."

Miss Copley tells a wonderful story of the time Chloe got herself into trouble, but Sasha behaved like the aristocratic Golden she knew she was. Miss Copley and her friend kept a caravan by the sea, and Chloe and Sasha provided some very memorable entertainment. Going out for a walk with visitors one day, Miss Copley was proud that she could trust the dogs not to touch a large cream cake they had left on the table.

"Well," Miss Copley told me, "we went back to the caravan, and there was Chloe sitting on a seat at the table, with her face covered in cream and jam. Sasha was sitting at the opposite end looking very autocratic and snooty, as if to say: 'I don't know anything about it, it certainly wasn't me!'. I just wished I had a camera with me! It was a comedy double act, with Sasha playing the straight man."

Graham and Brenda Hall have a very sad example of the friendship that can develop between animals. They had eight Goldens living at home until Naomi developed a rare cancer and died. She left behind two particularly close friends, Toby and Sheba, and her death was very obviously hard for these two dogs to bear.

"It was clear that Toby and Sheba were grieving; they tended to stay very close together after their loss," said Brenda. "Toby was the nicest, gentlest person that I have ever met, but twelve weeks after Naomi's death, he had a simple non-life-threatening operation and he never came out of the anaesthetic.

"The night Toby had his operation, Sheba was very upset. She wanted to fuss, wanted to sit on my lap. I just couldn't console her. We were all worried that Toby was having an operation, but we didn't know what was upsetting Sheba so much. Then we had a phone call to say that Toby had died under the anaesthetic. Sheba just went to pieces. She wouldn't go for a walk – the only place she would go was to her brother and sister's grave, that's all."

Graham and Brenda were extremely worried and had all sorts of tests done because Sheba appeared to be so ill. Finally, they managed to entice her out for a walk and on the way back her head went down and her feet started to drag. It was as if she was saying, 'well I'm on my own now'. Sheba went home and never left the house again.

Shortly after that, Sheba went to sleep and into a coma, and she didn't wake up. The vet was convinced that she had died of a broken heart. There was no physical evidence that there was anything wrong with her. All three died within a few months of one-another – that's how close Goldens can be.

You will meet, within the following pages, many 'dumb animals' who aren't as dumb as you may think. They are animals who enrich the lives of human beings – often quite consciously.

The bond of love between animals and humans

The Seekers Trust is a spiritual organisation which works to uplift the world using positive thought and love. They are particularly interested in improving the lot of animals on earth. In their book, 'A Pilgrimage with the Animals', we are told that animals can perceive the *real* you:

"In fact, you can judge yourselves by studying their attitudes towards you. If the results are not flattering, then change your own attitudes to life, and the animals will react more favourably to the change. They cannot be bluffed, as all true animal lovers know. They love you, dislike you, or distrust you because you cannot hide yourselves from them."

It was with great interest, then, that I read a letter from Dorothy Hawtin in response to my own letter in 'Country Life' which asked for stories about Goldens.

Dorothy told me about Gemma, a Golden Retriever who lives with friends about a mile away from her home. Ever since she was a puppy, Gemma has always shown the greatest affection for Dorothy and would start to bark and make a peculiar whistling whine as soon as she heard the sound of her car.

Gemma has to be restrained while Dorothy gets seated, and then there is an enormous reunion scene with Dorothy quietly talking to her while the dog rubs her head on her knee, and sometimes puts one of her enormous paws on her lap too.

I spoke to Biddy Thornton who is Gemma's owner: "It's quite amazing – no-one else receives the welcome Gemma gives to Dorothy. They have known each other since Gemma was a puppy and their relationship is just incredible."

Biddy told me that Gemma had puppies a few years ago, and she took herself into a cupboard under the stairs and refused to come out. She was really quite worried about her. Then Dorothy arrived and both ladies had tears of relief in their eyes when Gemma rushed out to greet her.

"She knows the sound of Dorothy's car and waits at the door for her to arrive. Dorothy is rather fragile but Gemma seems to understand. Although she goes absolutely scatty, Gemma knows not to barge into her. She just adores Dorothy."

"Kodi" (Ambrosia's Golden Kodiak Bear)

20

Rudy, Jane & Pruella of Davern

19

Linking hearts and minds

Barbara Woodhouse, the late famous and formidable doyenne of good animal behaviour, truly contended that animals possess the gift of telepathy, and that it is possible to develop a mutually receptive telepathic link with our pets.

John tells me that our four are at the front door and waiting for me at least five minutes before I arrive home in the car. I don't think they can hear the car when it's over three miles away.

It's the same with John: I always know when to put the dinner on because the dogs assemble at the front door. Interestingly, John does not have a nine-to-five job, so his arrival is not a time-based routine.

John recently came to collect me from the railway station but the train was twenty minutes late. Sam and Prudence waited in the car with him. Five minutes before the train pulled into the station, John tells me Prudence went scatty with excitement. I could see two sets of beautiful black eyes and two black noses in rapturous anticipation the second I walked through the station door.

Chappie practices communicating the other way. You can literally see him sending telepathic messages. If he's waiting for a titbit, then Chappie will sit, not too close, and narrow his eyes. You can see the rhythm of the thought signals as he says, "don't forget I'm here – don't give it all to the others."

He often stands in front of me to project his message in my direction. Sometimes he wants me to freshen the water in his bowl; on other occasions he thinks an extra-curricular walk might be in order. And then there's the gate into the grassy part of the garden: he's not allowed in when it's raining, but sometimes the deprivation is too hard for him to bear, and he has to ask for special permission. I look at him and try to tune into him, and we soon discover what it is that Chappie wants.

Brenda Hall told me of her remarkable bitch, Sansue Wanda of Stirchley, known affectionately as Tara, who was a proven mind reader: "One day my mother came to me and asked if I was going to the shop. I answered yes, why? My mother said she thought so, because Tara was sitting at the front door in readiness.

"We decided to conduct a little experiment to see whether it was telepathy, or whether Tara was simply reading the signs," Brenda said. "The next day I merely thought about going to the shop, but I didn't make any of the signs that Tara could associate with. I didn't put my coat on, I didn't get my bag – I just thought 'now I'm going to the shop'. True enough, Tara was sitting at the front door waiting for me."

Shirley Phillips of the San Roque Hotel in Birmingham told me about Leasha who had an uncanny sixth sense. When out in the car, for example, Leasha always knew when they were about to stop and have a run. "It didn't matter whether we were going to Chester from Birmingham or Northampton," she said. "Leasha wasn't able to tell we were there by memorising the road, because we came at the place from different directions. She never seemed to look out of the window to get the clues, either.

"In fact, she would start anticipating a stop five minutes before we got to the place. At home, we never had to use the word 'walkie', either. Leasha always seemed to know without anyone making any signs or fetching the lead.

"My daughter Wendy and her boyfriend Ian were doggie sitting one weekend. Leasha was sitting at the top of the stairs, and Wendy and Ian were sitting in the lounge. Wendy said, 'shall we take her now, or take her later', and Ian suggested they take her straight away. They turned round, and there was Leasha in front of them ready to go."

Alexis

Good Time Girl

Goldsmill Alexis is a good time girl, a daughter of Show Champion Westley Munro of Nortonwood who has inherited the twinkle from her father's eyes. "She just seems to worm her way into everyone's heart," says Pat Cooper, Alex's owner. "She's here to make the most of life and not worry about anything. To Alex, everything is just fun."

Alex speaks with her eyes: two deep meaningful pools of warmth and affection that seem to make her friends wherever she goes. "Alex is very laid back," says Pat. "It's tempting to believe that she has no brains – she's useless at retrieving. You throw the ball for her and she will pick it up if you insist, but she's just at likely to throw it back at you as if to say 'I can't think any further than fetching it'!"

Alex has earned the reputation in the neighbourhood as the naughty one: Dixie, Ria, Carly and Zoe are thought to be the good girls in the family.

"The problem," says Pat, "is that I'm always calling Alex when we're out for a walk. She's not naughty at all, she just has to go and say hello to everyone. We could be on the other side of the park and she will see someone come in, and charge off to meet them. Then she lies down, emotionally blackmailing people to rub her belly. She gets quite upset if they don't stop and make a fuss of her.

"Of course, if anyone has a bag, Alex has her nose in it, or in their pocket. No-one ever seems to mind because she's such fun to be around. It's those eyes: you could forgive anyone anything if they had eyes like that."

21

Alexis - Goldsmill Alexis

22

Barney (Streamrise Todu ex Prudence Going Gold - Stolford line)

Barney

A job for a real man

Barney and his handler are two boys together. You couldn't invent a more idyllic lifestyle for two incredibly brave men. All the ingredients are there: action, adventure, danger, heroics, teamwork . . . but why do they call Barney 'Doombrain'?

To call Barney a character would be an understatement. In the words of his handler, "He's a lunatic, absolutely puddled. Barney is nine years old and he's never grown up. In fact, he is totally loopy!"

Not so loopy, though, that Barney cannot be trusted to find explosives without touching them! Find but not touch – what a feat! Barney is a working police dog who carries out the vital but dangerous task of sniffing out bombs. When he finds them he jumps backwards and starts spinning like a top.

Barney started life with a young married couple who had spent a small fortune 'doing up' their home. He ate the kitchen. Barney was not the most popular of dogs: he was very very boisterous and very very bored – a round peg in a square hole. "I was looking for a special kind of dog," his handler told me, "so I had him on trial. At first, the stupid thing had no idea how to jump; it took him about ten days to realise he could actually get his feet off the ground."

Thankfully, Barney responded well to training – today he is *fit*, and described as a natural search dog. "One minute he's being totally loopy, and the next he can be very gentle and sedate. That's what I like about him: you can make him go, and make him calm down; he's got drive. We've worked in glass crystal factories, at antique fairs and in stately homes, and he can be trusted not to barge in like a bull in a china shop."

(Ahem, there is one little matter concerning Barney's love of cuddly toys which came to the fore when he was asked to check a girls' dormitory for bombs. His handler watched with amazement as Barney leapt into the dorm and jumped on each of the forty beds in turn, throwing cuddly toys into the air. It took some while to put the room back together again! I believe that the name 'Doombrain' has its origins in this day.)

To begin with, Barney was with the West Midlands Police, working loose through Birmingham city centre with traffic and people about, and there were no problems. In urban environments he is extremely good.

Now that he has transferred to Norfolk, Barney is having to adapt to wide open fields. One minute he will be as good as gold, the next his nose will have scented something and, whoosh, he's gone. "Barney is great because he is an independent soul with initiative and intelligence," says his handler. "He also has a stubborn streak in him, and gets carried away by his nose when we are in open spaces. Sometimes I could brain him!"

Barney is now being trained to adjust to his new freedom. "We have to recreate the problem we have, but in an environment where he cannot abscond. There's little point in training in the middle of a 200 acre field because he could just disappear. Instead, we start on a smaller scale and gradually increase the distance. You cannot afford to stage a training exercise that you, the handler, are not going to win."

Meanwhile, Barney enjoys the dual pleasures of plenty of exercise – both physical and mental – and a happy home life with his handler and family. "Barney is a central part of the family, although he lives in a kennel because he just doesn't like a centrally heated house.

"I could literally take Barney anywhere with me," says his handler. "We've just lectured and demonstrated to 150 Brownies, and he went to a big convention of the Women's Institute a few days ago. I let him into the hall – and he wasn't at all what they expected. He ran up and down the aisles, across the stage, and charged in amongst them. He thought it was great. He's a pest, a real character, and a confounded nuisance!"

He is also a hero.

The Perfect Companion

23

Molly

Golden Retrievers are the third most popular breed in the United Kingdom, coming after Jack Russells and Labradors in number. Whilst there are usually some 16,000 Retrievers registered with the Kennel Club in Britain each year, I am told that there are nearer to 80,000 registered in America.

Although there is usually a long waiting list to 'rescue' a Golden in the UK, the problem of over-population in the States is severe. Yankee Golden Retriever Rescue provides medical services and boarding for abandoned Golden Retrievers until adoptive homes can be found. Ann Bonner was first introduced to the Rescue when a temporary home needed to be found for Molly, a seven year old Golden who had been turned out because she was too old to produce any more puppies.

"Our decision to say 'yes', was the beginning of one of the most wonderful relationships we ever had with a dog," says Ann. "Molly had only been with us for a week before we fell in love with her. We became her long-term adoptive home and she became an integral part of our family."

Molly was a very special Golden. She had been uprooted from her home, taken to an animal hospital, spayed, poked and prodded, and then plonked down in a new environment with people and animals she had never met. "Yet from the first day," says Ann, "she accepted each of us without a grumble."

Molly had many wonderful qualities which endeared her to the Bonner family. The first was her resilience and trust. Although she gave indications of having been abused (cringing if anyone quickly raised their hand high, spoke loudly, or carried an object over her), she was friendly and gentle with all.

Second was her devotion. Ann tells me that Molly treated her as if she was the best, most important thing in the world. Happiness to Molly was simply being by her side. In fact, the family nicknamed her 'Velcro' as she was always near Ann – and Ann loved it!

Molly's affection was legendary. She enjoyed both giving and receiving it. From toddlers to strollers grabbing her ear or tail and patting her on the head, to home-bound elderly folk gently stroking her while reminiscing, Molly sat quietly, giving an occasional lick or nudge of encouragement for them to continue.

And her behaviour was exemplary. "We could and did take Molly everywhere," said Ann. Molly visited nursing homes (where she had her own clients), calmed students' pre-exam jitters at the college where Ann works, and introduced very young children to the world of dogs by patiently enduring their first attempts at interaction. She went to baseball and football games, to work, to the woods, to dinner with friends: her attitude was always that of patience, tolerance, and unobtrusive friendliness.

Ann is now a member of the Board of Directors and totally committed to the Yankee Golden Retriever Rescue, and she says that Molly is the reason. "Senior Goldens make wonderful adoptive pets," says Ann. "They usually get along with other dogs, they are great nannies for the lonely only dog, and make a nice addition to multi-dog households."

Because they are gentle and tolerant, these older Goldens are excellent at introducing children to the world of dogs. Seniors are less work than puppies and young dogs as they are housebroken and have outgrown the furniture reconstruction stage. This doesn't mean that slippers and socks will cease to disappear – but they will be in one piece when you find them!

These calm, dignified Goldens will not jump on Great Aunt Ethel or topple an unsteady toddler. Vigorous exercise is not required; sedate walks will do just fine. They are happy to do anything, go anywhere, as long as it's with their special someone. And they are ideal companions for apartment dwellers, senior citizens, and families who haven't the time for puppy training.

Although Molly is gone now, Ann says that what she taught the family about love, gentleness, and the true Golden spirit remains. "Although her passing was painful for us and her stay much too short, we wouldn't trade the time we had with her for ANYTHING!"

Bear

24

Friendship with other animals

Bear was found in ill health on Rye Beach, New Hampshire. He was scheduled for euthanasia after his legal holding time expired, but the Yankee Golden Retriever Rescue was able to spare him. Based on the condition of his teeth, it was determined that Bear was approximately six years old. He was grossly overweight at 110 pounds and he had one eyelid that required surgery. YGRR had the surgery done and started him on a strict weight loss diet. Once on the mend, Bear was put up for adoption.

With their daughter Keri grown and starting college, Dale and Karen Broadbent filed an application for a Rescue Golden Retriever. The Rescue requires that all potential adoptive owners be screened to ensure the best possible homes for displaced Goldens. Once approved, Dale and Karen visited the kennel to make their selection.

The Broadbent's criteria was somewhat unique since they already had two Angora rabbits as house pets and they were looking for a dog that wouldn't threaten them. Even at his reduced weight of 93 pounds, Bear was still the largest dog in the kennel. "Despite his size," says Dale, "we felt that he was the best choice out of the ten or so dogs we saw. His personality seemed calmer than the other dogs, even though he had been there for nearly three months."

The first few days were anxious, since Karen had never been around dogs and was a bit intimidated by Bear's size. To ensure a smooth transition for the rabbits, Dale and Karen left them in their cages in the kitchen for the first few days. Bear was able to sniff the rabbits and watch them as they moved in their cages, and after this adjustment period, he was introduced to them over a period of several days with Bear on the leash and the rabbits running freely around the room.

"It took only a few corrections to show Bear that the rabbits were not supper or toys," says Dale. "Within two weeks Bear was off the leash with the rabbits running freely in the house. Now the rabbits jump over Bear's nose as he lies on the floor and Bear doesn't even look up."

Bear's health was good for the first few months in his new home, but then he developed severe diarrhoea. Several diet changes and visits to the vets failed to identify the source of the problem. After a month with little or no change in Bear's condition, Dale and Karen took Bear to a major veterinary hospital where he was admitted for five days.

When they picked up Bear, Dale and Karen were told he had terminal cancer. With chemotherapy, he might live four months; without it, only two. They chose not to subject him to the chemotherapy and decided to make his last days as comfortable as possible. A high fibre dog food stopped the diarrhoea and he was fed up to seven times a day. The couple also took him to the office with them so that he didn't have to be alone.

Benji

Four months later Dale and Karen called the vet to say that not only was Bear still alive, but he had gained ten pounds and showed no signs of illness except for occasional bouts of diarrhoea. She called them back soon after to apologise – the pathologist has misread the tests. Bear didn't have cancer, he had an inflammatory bowel disease which could be controlled by diet. "Needless to say," Dale said, "by this time, Bear was thoroughly spoiled and overweight!"

Dale and Karen have been owned by Bear for three and a half years now, and they love him. "He doesn't know he's a dog," says Karen. "In fact he doesn't particularly like other dogs – we suspect it's jealousy. He will not fetch and doesn't know what to do with a tennis ball. He goes to extremes to avoid any form of water, and will even cross over the street if we approach a lawn sprinkler."

"Like all Goldens," Dale adds, "Bear is an attention addict. Once you start petting him he will stay forever and will nudge your arm every time you stop!"

Bear certainly landed on all four paws the day he wandered onto Rye Beach.

The Congregational Golden

Benji is a 14-year-old 'people person', an honorary member of the Leigh Road Baptist Church at Leigh-on-Sea in Essex. His owner, Joy Bawtree, says, "Benji isn't really interested in other dogs; it's people that interest him."

Benji is a heartily welcomed visitor at the church coffee morning every Thursday. "The old folks simply adore him," Joy says. "He dashes in with his woollen doll in his mouth and plonks it on peoples' laps. This goes on for about an hour; he has to speak to everyone. Then when the speaker addresses the congregation and we pray together, Benji lies down very quietly with his head on his paws – he's quite a character."

A social butterfly at heart, Benji also accompanies Joy's lay-preacher husband, Edgar, to children's services, helps Joy in her counselling role at the church, and goes with Joy to visit friends in hospital. "Benji is made particularly welcome at the hospice because he is very gentle, albeit very big. He has a wonderful way of looking at people and will curl up with them as close to their legs as he can get."

Despite his hectic social life, Benji has only ever had one illness, a problem with his ears. "At fourteen, he's still an absolute delight," says Joy, "full of vim and vigour. The vet is delighted with him as he's still slim with no rheumatics."

Joy believes that cod liver oil (every day from October until March), and plenty of vegetables with his meal each evening, have helped keep Benji young and healthy. "I'm very strict with him," she says. "He doesn't get titbits."

Benji is so much in love with Joy that he watches her every move. If Joy goes out without him, then Benji rushes upstairs to find a piece of her clothing or a slipper, and rests his head upon it until she returns.

"We are absolutely inseparable," she concludes. "Yes! I adore him, but on a one-to-one basis, we treat each other with great respect and very much love and care."

Benji went quietly to sleep in December 1993, at a great age and having lived a great life.

An animal's intuition

It took Merryn Wells-Burr from Chard in Somerset five years to convince her husband that they should have a Golden Retriever, and only one visit to 'view' before they came home with a tiny bundle of joy called Tamara. "From that moment on," says Merryn, "life has been full of loving Golden moments."

"Tammy was very easy to train and is very sensitive to the people around her," says Merryn. "Her devotion is illustrated by her behaviour when my daughter was expecting her first child: Tammy started jumping over a 6ft fence to go to my daughter's home a few blocks away. Her motherly instinct seemed to sense that my daughter needed attention.

"Tammy was very restless the day my grandson came home from hospital; in fact, she wouldn't settle until she actually saw the baby. She would gently watch my daughter to see if she was caring for the baby to her expectations, and then she settled down to become a great friend to our grandson.

"Then came the day when Tammy started jumping the fence again. I didn't have to be told that my daughter was expecting another child, and she was of course!"

Benji

25

Hayley, Tammy & Billy

26

A son of Davern Figaro in Sweden with Friends

One evening, when Merryn was at training classes with Tammy, the trainer asked whether she might know someone who could re-home a Labrador. The Labrador turned out to be a Golden Retriever called Billy. He was very thin when he came to his new home, very confused, and very disruptive.

"Quite frankly, I didn't realise what I was taking on with Billy. It took me six weeks to get him to respond to me. We had to show him what to do by telling Tammy to do it, and then Billy copied her. But he had a mind of his own: he wouldn't lie down when I told him, even though he knew what was expected of him. He had to go where he wanted to go, and he certainly wouldn't let anyone cuddle him.

"My daughter persevered and insisted he had a cuddle, and in the end he liked nothing better than the company of humans. Our withdrawn boy started to be the first in the queue when it came to brushing and trimming."

Billy also graduated from being an obstreperous Golden to a star in the obedience ring. "He could retrieve dumb bells and scent, and he became an exemplary PAT Dog," says Merryn. " He was a very boisterous dog, but as soon as we walked into the old folks' home he became very quiet and calm. He used to smile at the nurses by rolling his lips up, but not at the old people in case he frightened them."

As a step-father, Billy sparkled. "When Tammy had her puppies Billy's character really came out," says Merryn. "The morning after they were born he asked to go and see Tammy. Tammy was so pleased to show off her babies, and Billy gave a great big smile when he saw them. The puppies used him as a big hot water bottle, curling up with him to keep warm at night."

Merryn kept one of Tammy's daughters from the litter and Billy, Tammy and Haley became firm friends. "All three used to carry my parcels home when we went shopping and there was always someone who stopped us and wanted to stroke them."

Billy came to live with Merryn when he was two, and he died at the age of seven. "We only had him for a short time," said Merryn, "but he was such an angel, such a darling boy. I miss him very much. There's certain music that I can't play any more because it always brings tears to my eyes. We used to listen to it together, when we had our Golden moments."

Calico

28

Golden etiquette

Mike and Jackie Grubb live in the USA. It is often said that the British are real animal lovers, but it has been my experience that American people equal, and often surpass, our kindness. Like many Golden Retriever owners, Mike and Jackie view their animals as people with unique personalities. Whilst they take part in shows, field trials and obedience competitions, the Grubbs believe that the dogs' temperaments are by far the most important factor.

Gypsy became their first Golden in 1973, and he cheerfully entered show, obedience and field competitions with them. One of his highlights occurred in 1978 when, as a team member, he won the BOB (Best of Breed) award for the top Golden handler in New England. His long life over thirteen years was, according to Mike, due to being surrounded by chicks.

Gypsy was joined by Sunshine, a wild field girl, and Blossom, a cute and biddable lady. The three took great delight in performing their function of Golden Alarm Clocks. Later, the Grubbs shared their lives with Harry and Wally. When Wally died of cancer at the tender age of four, Mike and Jackie were heartbroken, and many of their friends in the Golden Retriever world shared their sorrow. But it is the times of happiness that remain forever. The latest member of the Grubb family is Calico, a two-year-old terror who uncannily displays many of Wally's endearing traits. Mike told me, "Calico loves to play ball and, of the many stuffed animals we have in the house for them to play with, she rummages through the pile with her nose until she finds the monkey Wally took with him through his chemotherapy treatments. Then she carries it around with her."

Wally

31

30

Blossom - (Wildwood Dakmount Blossom CD)

29

Harry and Wally - (Bon Vue Dakmount Herriot & Bon Vue Dakmount Wallingford)

Mike writes beautifully, and so he describes Blossom's house training escapades in his own words:

We picked up Blossom from Massachusetts on December 23, and returned to our log home in central New Hampshire for a New England Christmas. Because of the cold weather, Blossom spent the first two months inside our house, venturing outside only once or twice for a few minutes. Although she was very good about using her papers, by the time she was four months old we decided enough was enough and the time for housebreaking had arrived.

"The weather and time of year could not have been worse. Blossom was born in late October, her four-month birthday fell in late February, when snow depth was near its maximum and winter retained a firm grip on New England. To make matters worse, this was the year of the 'Blizzard of '78,' and the snow pack around our house exceeded six feet in many places.

"These were the conditions that Blossom and I faced together. Her housebreaking became a matter of determining if, when I noticed her nervous circling, I could thrust my feet into heavy boots, throw on a coat, scoop up Blossom and be out the door before it was too late. We usually made it, although my wild antics, including a not too infrequent slip and sprawl in the snow, often caused Blossom to forget all about relieving herself. Whether this was because she was now scared to death, thought this was a new game, or perhaps that her master had finally gone crazy, I never knew.

"Once outside, I would stand in the sub-zero weather and biting wind while Blossom rolled, chased squirrels or watched the chickadees on the feeders until the urge returned, this often requiring as long as fifteen minutes. Following her anticipated performance and exuberant praise from me, we would return to the house, Blossom to spread her snow on the floor while I thawed by the wood stove.

"Blossom learned easily and we later discovered this snowy experience affected her in an unusual way. As spring slowly returned and the snow receded, Blossom would religiously relieve herself while standing in a patch of snow. As early May rolled around, the only snow left was a small area located on the north side of the house. If Blossom was playing in the snow-free meadow below the house, she would suddenly race the 100 yards to squat in this snow patch.

"We wondered what would happen when this area too melted, but Blossom had that problem solved. When the morning of no snow arrived, Blossom took a quick look around and headed for the small ditch along our road which carried the runoff from the melting snow. Remembering that her feet were always cold when she was trained to do her business outdoors, Blossom stood with all four feet in the icy water and, giving us that smug Golden look, made her own liquid contribution to the ditch.

"How can you not love them?"

Candy and Bear

Susan Rezy had Boxers for twenty years and Malamutes for fifteen years before she was acquired by Candy, the Golden Retriever. "Candy was quite a change, and quite a shock," says Susan. "I assumed that being a Retriever she would retrieve birds. She didn't, but she did retrieve shoes, pine cones, litter, the mail and – her very favourite which she usually saved for when company came over – dirty laundry!"

Despite her avaricious proclivities, Candy was Susan's first perfect puppy. "Candy was the perfect companion," Susan told me. "She was quiet when you wanted her to be and ready to go as soon as she heard the jingle of car keys. She was always a big hit when she went to visit my Mother and Grandmother at the nursing home; wheelchairs never bothered her and she knew how to stay out from under the residents' walkers.

"Candy died prematurely when she was seven. We have missed her a great deal – she showed us how golden their personalities truly are. She has been a very hard act to follow."

Bear, the cute blonde puppy in the picture, has grown into a cute blonde adult. "Bear was and is the busiest dog I've ever had," said Susan. "He is always ready to do anything. In fact, he's always doing something. His most favourite toy is what we call a boing boing ball. He adores it and plays with it all day. He even sleeps with it and takes it in the van when we go places."

Bear's other passion is tracking and he's managed to get Susan hooked on tracking too. "We started him when he was seven months old and Bear learned much faster than I did. At nine months he was certified by a tracking judge, which meant that he was ready to take an actual tracking test. Shortly after his first birthday, Bear passed the test and got his tracking degree. He is now officially known as Pinecrest's Linebacker TD. We're now working in the field, and as usual he's far ahead of me."

Susan says that Bear's sheer joy in living makes it impossible for her to ever get mad at him and, anyway, he never does anything wrong. "Bear is only two-and-a-half years old and I really look forward to all the adventures we have yet to experience together," Susan says.

32

Candy and Bear

Cinamon

the agility champ

Cinamon found it extremely difficult when she was learning agility. "Most dogs like doing agility," says Gillian Clark, Cinamon's owner, "but Saffy, as we call her, is a bit of a wimp, to tell you the truth. But we persevered, and it was very good for her in the end. It changed her character, brought her out of herself and gave her confidence."

Saffy has eight sisters and, like all large families, there is a tendency to vie for attention and compete with one-another to become the apple of mummy's eye. "I try and give all the girls something to do to make them special," says Gillian, "otherwise the quieter ones might get left out."

Gillian and her girls are all very keen on agility, preferring it to obedience or breed showing (although some of them try their paws at these pastimes too). "One of the things about agility is that you can have a tremendous amount of fun without having to get to the top," Gillian says.

"When we first went into agility, my initial aim was to get the dog to actually use the equipment. Then my aim was to keep her in the ring and stop her going to visit all the people round the ring. Then we set our sights on getting her round without knocking a jump down – there are lots of personal achievements you can aim for, and be very pleased with yourself when you succeed.

"Believe me, if you have 250 dogs in a class, it's quite something to get a place. Even 25th place is something to be proud of. If you take part in an elementary competition, you win a clear round rosette if you get round the course in time and keep all the equipment up – so even relative beginners can go home with a prize. You can have a good time with your dog, and keep both of you fit – it's great fun."

Gillian believes that you have to be very careful when training Golden Retrievers. "You could have a dog that's wonderful at seven months old and gives up when she's eight months old if you are too heavy handed," she says. "That's what happened with my first dog. She was very bright but I was very badly advised about her training. She had enough character to tell me to get it myself when I asked her to retrieve a dumb bell!

"I don't think you should start serious training with the average Golden Retriever until it is a year old. Instead, I spend time teaching my puppies how to live at home with me. At 12 or 15 months you can teach them a tremendous amount in a very short time because they can now concentrate and this makes everything very much easier for you both.

"I'm glad to say that trainers are beginning to recognise that the old style of training is entirely unsuitable for most dogs, but certainly for Golden Retrievers. They don't want to be regimented, thank you."

Now approaching the grand age of eleven, Cinamon is thinking about retiring from this hectic sport, but she is leaving a bequest to encourage any up-and-coming hopefuls. "We are going to have the Cinamon Shield," says Gillian. "It will, of course, have a rat on it."

A rat?

"Well," Gillian explained, "when Cinamon was first starting, I had to find a way to encourage her over the equipment and a 'magic mouse' proved to be the perfect incentive. Cinamon would do anything to get hold of that mouse. It went before her over the A frame, ahead of her over the jumps – and everyone who knows Cinamon remembers what we call 'that damn rat'. Even when Cinamon has gone, her story will be there, on the back of the trophy."

Sunny keeps dry

35

Sunny and Jolly

36

Rudy & Flavella

34

Wall-to-wall Golden Retrievers

If you stand up at Charles and Brenda Lowe's house, you have a good chance of losing your seat to a Golden Retriever! There are currently seventeen Golden Retrievers sharing Meadowcroft, home of the famous Davern Goldens. It was once remarked that the Lowes don't really need a carpet with so many Golden Retrievers to add warmth and comfort to the home.

Take a look at your own Golden's pedigree. The chances are that the name Davern will appear at least once. Chappie, Samson, Sophie, Oliver and Prudence can all boast the famous Champion Davern Figaro as part of their ancestry, and jolly glad we are for it, too.

"Figaro really was a great character," says Brenda Lowe. "We used to call him Sunny because life was so full of happiness and fun. He loved everybody: adults, children, other dogs and puppies, and you just had to look at him to feel happy inside."

Sunny was also a real Retriever: "He used to love stealing clothes from the bathroom," says Brenda; "he'd often be caught parading around the garden with an illicit pair of pants!

"His sense of humour came to the fore the first time I took him to do his show gun dog qualifier," Brenda said. "He went out to hunt, picked up the scent, found his pheasant, started back ... and then he looked at me and the spectators, and I could see he thought it was all a huge joke. He threw the pheasant in the air and rolled on it – and he did it all the more when everybody started to laugh and clap. Figaro was just a show off. He brought a crumpled bird back eventually, but he left me with a very red face. We had to go back the next year and do it properly!"

Brenda believes that Sunny inherited his happy character from his mother, although she is quick to point out that his father, Champion Camrose Tallyrand of Anbria, was a special dog too. "Like Tallyrand, Sunny's greatest joy was to get a crowd of young puppies running around the garden and playing with him. Tallyrand even appeared in a television advertisement with lots of puppies when he was twelve years old.

"Sunny's mother, Champion Camrose Pruella of Davern, was a terrific character who could speak in any language. When we entertained visitors from abroad, Mandy as we called her, would speak to them in these loud yodelling tones: 'woo woo woo'. You could understand exactly what she was saying, wherever you came from.

"Some people don't like to see Goldens in fancy dress but Sunny and Mandy used to adore dressing up. We used to put a little head scarf on Mandy so she could wear it to greet people, and she absolutely loved it, she was so proud of herself."

Sunny - Ch. Davern Figaro (Ch. Camrose Tallyrand of Ambria ex Ch. Camrose Pruella of Davern)

Show Champion Amirene King Eider of Davern is another of the Davern personalities: "Ky greets everyone by carrying their arm in his mouth. He's a very busy dog who is interested in everything and everyone, but he's slightly accident prone because he does everything at a gallop. If the Goldens go swimming, it's always Keider in first, setting off to swim the channel."

Polo – or Twilly Apollo of Davern to you – is Keider's accomplice in crime: "Goldens love to grab people," says Brenda. "Sometimes they grab your clothes, and sometimes they actually nip you. The results can be quite amusing, especially if the person is wearing a bathrobe or a towel.

"Once, Polo and Keider grabbed a lady visitor as she came out of the bathroom. Polo grabbed her dressing gown and Keider got hold of her arm. She wasn't used to Goldens, so she thought she was being attacked and she didn't dare move. She stood there absolutely petrified

until her daughter, my kennel maid, walked in and told her that the two boys were just being friendly."

Champion Sutton Rudy was the Lowe's first Golden, and the first member of the family to have been misunderstood. "Rudy used to smile so broadly that sometimes people thought he was snarling. Visitors would jump back in alarm until I told them not to worry, that he was only laughing at them. You could get Rudy to smile to order."

Show Champion Verdayne Dandini of Davern, whose pet name was Dixie, used to break the ice with his 'party piece' by pinching a box of chocolate mints off the table and offering them to visitors when they called. "We always used to say that Dixie sold his puppies for us by snuggling up to people," says Brenda. "He would sit on their laps, roll over, and give his paw to them – especially if it was a child." But how do the Lowes get on with seventeen Goldens in the house?

"Well," says Brenda, "Charles often asks if there's any room for him to sit down, or should he just go and sit in the kennel? His dogs lie at his feet, whereas mine come and sit on the settee with me. We have to work very hard to try not to have favourites because some characters are more assertive than others. We make a point of bringing the quieter ones to us for cuddles because they love it so much.

"The oldies can be quite amusing when it comes to finding a seat in the home. They stand and look at a chair if it's occupied by another dog, and then they look at me and say, 'tell him to get off mummy, that's my chair'. Golden Oldies are very special characters: they want it all their own way, but in a very nice, endearing, sort of way.

Seventeen Golden Retrievers now *that's* my idea of heaven!

Saved by love

Champion Darris Double Diamond, known affectionately by his friends as Dexter, or 'Decky Dog', is loved throughout the Golden Retriever world for his beauty, bounding enthusiasm, and an acute sense of humour, witnessed by his propensity to 'play to the gallery' at Crufts and other championship shows. "Dexter would just wait for the applause," says his owner Connie Gray, "and in return the audience would be waiting for him to do something naughty. He rarely disappointed them."

At ten years of age, Dexter was still winning, and was judged the top veteran dog at the Golden Retriever Club Show. Connie decided that Dexter would then retire on a high note, at the top. In his latter years, both Connie and Dexter are enjoying a new freedom away from the ring, and not minding too much if he tears through the bracken and undergrowth, threatening to spoil his thick coat.

Connie says that just before Christmas, her four grandsons were playing Monopoly on the floor and the game became very 'zippy' when they lost the dice. There were accusations of 'you've got it', and frantic searching. "Dexter was almost beside himself with excitement," says Connie. "He ran into the garden, collected his big squeaky dice, and dashed back into the lounge and threw it onto the board. There was such laughter and squeals of delight, and of course, Dexter ate some Monopoly money for an encore."

38

Ch. Darris Double Diamond and Darris Double Dazzler of Chessgold

Dexter is 'one of the boys', remaining firmly at the centre of the action whenever Connie's grandsons come to visit. "I'm often asked to please take Dexter indoors," Connie says, "as he stops the ball before it goes into the goal, or takes up the cricket stumps in the middle of the game. Then, late at night, they all troop upstairs to bed, followed by Dexter of course!"

But Dexter is a star for his sensitivity, as well as his sense of fun and ring appeal: "A close neighbour was terribly ill," says Connie. "He hadn't been given long to live and was spending eighteen hours each day sitting in an oxygen tent. As you can imagine, our friend was extremely depressed and had practically lost the will to live.

"Dexter used to visit the gentleman every day and insisted upon treating him as normal, rather than as an invalid. I could see that Dexter was quite literally pulling out all the stops for this man. He would grab his slippers and eat his grapes, and generally dash around being a clown with a busy tail and a smile on his face. The two began to look forward to seeing each other every day, and gradually our friend started to get better.

"Eventually, it got to the stage where Selby left his oxygen tent behind, got his own dog, and started going out for walks. Everyone was amazed by the recovery – but I know that animals can make a lot of difference when you are badly ill. Selby died two years later, but he had two last years of high quality living."

Like many Golden owners, Connie says that she feels privileged to have shared her life with her canine friend.

Connie sadly lost the great Champion Darris Double Diamond in January 1993. Although life felt bleak, Connie has welcomed a delightful little character called Jayne (NoJayne) into her life.

Big soft Digger

39

Digger

Digger doesn't like it when strange dogs talk to his mummy. "If I say hello to a dog when we're out on a walk," says Lini Grant from Northampton, "Digger gets quite upset. He's a very loyal, loving boy, and a great big baby. If there are only one or two dogs he will play with them, but if there are more, he gets quite frightened and hides behind my skirts."

If you think a dog can't talk, go and visit Digger Grant. "He talks with his eyes," says Lini. "He looks at me to get my attention, and then he looks at whatever it is he wants. At six o'clock in the evening he brings me his dinner bowl, as if to say, 'come on mum, fill that'. And when he's been left on his own for a short while, Digger gives us a good telling off when we arrive home: 'grrerr, nyom, grrrerr, nyom, nyom.'."

Digger's favourite pastime is chasing rabbits. "But they have to run away," says Lini, "or he just looks at them and comes scuttling back to me. He thinks I should go chasing rabbits with him: if I walk on, he rushes in front of me and sits down pleading with his eyes for me to follow him into the bushes. I think he's really quite frightened of them."

Digger does his fair share of the work in the house. "Digger is in charge of the telephone," says Lini. "If it rings while I'm out in the garden, he comes straight to me and barks to let me know. He doesn't do a lot of gardening these days, but he used to help when he was younger."

. . . I wondered why he was called Digger!

Sir Lancelot

Tilita Sir Lancelot shimmered with all that is good. He died not long ago, at the age of eleven. His loving owner, Michaela Edridge, says, "Doyle was my friend, implicitly. He was the best dog in the whole world; almost from birth I knew he was special."

Many of you will already know Doyle, star of television commercials and poster campaigns: he was a real pro, with his own agent and an extremely professional television manner.

Doyle only had to be told once," says Michaela. "He would do retake after retake on a shoot, because a puppy might have nipped him or started pushing about, but Doyle would automatically know what to do after one telling. For one commercial Doyle and his sister Dottie had to sit in front of a fire with two cats, and the Goldens behaved beautifully. The cats were another matter, and the agency had to resort to stuffed cats because the live ones just wouldn't stay in front of the fire!

"If the post arrived at home," Michaela continued, "you could tell Doyle to take a letter to Kaeti or to Lisa, and he knew exactly where to go and what to do. He seemed to be totally on your wavelength."

Doyle also helped when it came to finding new homes for young puppies. "Whenever people came to view a litter he used to show off and illustrate how great Golden Retrievers could be," says Michaela. "I didn't have to do

Doyle

40

anything except let him loose and everyone would want to buy him. I could have sold him a million times over – but he was more precious to me than money."

In the field of public relations, Doyle was an exemplary proponent of the Canine Kingdom. "Doyle was the finest PAT Dog visitor you could ever wish to meet," Michaela claims.

PAT Dogs (Pets As Therapy) is a charity which recognises that looking after people is not only a matter of making them well or keeping them well, but also of making them happy. PAT Dogs go straight through the barrier of loneliness by visiting the young, elderly and infirm, and cheering them up. To be accepted as a registered PAT Dog, he or she must pass a temperament test and be shown to have a friendly, happy and reliable disposition, as well as enjoying having a fuss made of him by different people.

"Some of the people Doyle visited had had pets all their lives," says Michaela, "so of course when Doyle went in, the floodgates really opened. He used to visit an elderly lady in a cancer hospice every week. She was a wonderful spirited old lady, who came to know the histories of all of my dogs. Doyle comforted her so much before she died. Another lady in the hospice died with a dog on her bed – you can imagine the comfort that must have brought."

Doyle also used to attend therapy sessions in a mental hospital, helping people to become accustomed to life in the community rather than large institutions: "Some of the patients were extremely frightened of dogs so we went for many weeks, gradually getting closer and closer until many of the patients were actually stroking and touching him. Doyle was so patient and understanding, he knew just when to put himself forward and when not to, almost as though he had been pre-conditioned."

To keep fit, Doyle enjoyed participating in agility sports. "You need someone with enthusiasm and character to succeed in agility," says Michaela, "and Doyle had the perfect personality. He would have made a fabulous working dog. He was a big strong boy who began to shine in obedience at a very young age – but if he decided he'd had enough, Doyle wouldn't think twice about sitting down in the middle of the field and telling me so."

On the retrieving front, Doyle's special trick was to fetch car tyres! He needed a human male accomplice to throw it for him, but Doyle could fetch it back with no problems. "He even managed to dig his tyre out of a 3ft snow drift, " says Michaela.

"Doyle didn't have the tiniest bit of aggression in him, yet as soon as there was any threat of anything dodgy, his hackles were up and he was standing by me protecting me. Sir Lancelot would be there, minus the white horse, but ready to defend me. When you lose so great a friend," Michaela says, "you have to concentrate on the fact that if you hadn't known them, your life would have been so very much poorer."

I Love Tracking

"I Love Tracking" this was the message conveyed to me by Ed and Marallyn Wight from Michigan, USA. And so do their Goldens! Hooked on the sport since 1972, and now well-known tracking judges, Ed and Marallyn are probably amongst the fittest people alive: a tracking test entails two days of extensive walking over varied terrain, and they do it a considerable number of times a year!

"Ed introduced our first Golden, Gena, to tracking when she was 10 weeks old, which was unheard of in 1972," says Marallyn. "People at that time generally felt that dogs should have all their other obedience titles before they began tracking. But Gena loved to track more than anything and still romped through a short fun track when she was past 13 years of age. Just the tick of our car's turn-indicator when we were driving on a country road turned her normally placid behaviour into a whirlwind of excitement. She always had hopes that we were going to turn off to let her go tracking!"

Gena, who was officially known as Kyrie Genever, American-Canadian UDTX, WC, (and not at all stuck-up despite her grand medals and gongs) was the first Golden to pass an American TDX at a National Golden Retriever Club of America Specialty. A pioneer in many senses, Gena used to help Ed and Marallyn when they were involved in experimental tracks which led to the development of the American Kennel Club's TDX.

At one of these, in Illinois, Ed and Gena were tracking in high cover. Ed, not being able to see Gena, realised suddenly that his lead was no longer taut. He cautiously followed it forward to where it disappeared into a large hole. "There was Gena," says Ed, "looking up at me from the bottom of a 6ft deep pit! I had to jump down into the pit to hoist her out, and she then went on to finish the track."

On another occasion, this time in Canada, Gena was chased off the track by a broom-wielding non-English speaking woman who didn't understand what Ed and Gena were doing! Perhaps we should add PDTO (Persistent Despite The Odds) to Gena's long list of achievements!

Marallyn's first Golden Retriever (two months younger than Gena) was Anthea of Setherwood American-Canadian UDTX. Thea, at two years of age, was the first Golden to earn two Canadian TDX, which was appropriate in as much as she was born in Canada. Thea was also involved in the experimental tracks which helped develop the American TDX. (The latter began several years after the Canadian TDX.)

41

Today, Ed and Marallyn share their lives with five Goldens: Mindy and Tovë, litter mates who reached the grand age of 14 in March 1993; Shane, aged seven; Ngaio, aged three; and puppy Christie, who has just started her tracking career. (More grandly, the four elders are known as Parabens Cinnamindy American-Canadian CDX, American TD, Canadian TDX; Parabens Tovë American-Canadian TD, Canadian CD; Kyrie Arcane Shane American-Canadian TDX; and Kyrie Caerfilly Ngaio American-Canadian TD.)

"Of the nine American and Canadian TDX titles our Goldens have earned to date," says Marallyn, "seven of those came as the only successful track of the day. We are proud and grateful to all our dear Goldens who have given us so much pleasure through their efforts."We always wonder why anyone would want another breed, but perhaps from a selfish standpoint, it's just as well that some do!"

Meanwhile, between tracking, judging, entertaining friends from out of state, and teaching in their training club, Ed and Marallyn still have time to be active members of the Golden Retriever Club of America and keep in touch with their children and grandchildren across continent!

Ed and Marallyn judge between five and 10 times a year, each event lasting for two days. They lay tracks for tests they aren't judging, and they often have the jobs of chairman or secretary for tests. "From time-to-time," says Marallyn, "we show our own dogs when they are ready and we're lucky enough to get drawn. Canada accepts entries on a 'first come, first served' basis, but the entries there are also limited in number. When we're training, we go out three or four times weekly, and perhaps a fifth time when we're about to show."

Here are two people who will never be able to say that life has been boring. And their Goldens were certainly in luck when the owners were handed out. (**For more information about tracking, see chapter 6.**)

42

Kyrie Caerfilly Ngaio Am-Can TD

43

Thea, Gena, Sloan, Mindy & Tovë (left to right) - The Wight Goldens

Earl – Sue's eyes

Fifteen per cent of the UK population believes a guide dog can tell the time, according to research conducted by the Guide Dogs for the Blind Association. Although 85 per cent of respondents were aware that guide dogs are trained to walk in a straight line unless there is an obstacle or they need to locate a pedestrian crossing, 92 per cent thought that it was the guide dog and not the owner who decides when to cross a road.

Fifty per cent of those questioned thought that a dog can be trained to tell the difference between red and green traffic lights, despite the fact that a dog's perception of colour is very limited. Nearly 40 per cent assumed that if a blind person has a guide dog, they never need assistance. This is not always the case. Did you know, for example, that when the harness handle is lowered onto the dog's back, the owner is indicating they would appreciate help? Interestingly, over 50 per cent of the respondents felt it appropriate to honk their horns or stop the car and wave a blind person across the road; 2 per cent would even flash their headlights!

44

Sue Davis and Earl

45

Gillian Batterham with Gypsy

FACTS ABOUT GUIDE DOGS

A person must be 16 before they apply for a guide dog. There is no upper age limit.

Each Guide Dog costs its owner just 50p; all after care is supported by GDBA, including food and veterinary bills.

The average working life of a guide dog is seven to eight years. One guide dog owner could need as many as 9 or 10 dogs in a lifetime.

You should never distract a working dog.

Never feed a guide dog – they have a balanced diet.

When driving, never stop along a road to let a guide dog owner cross unless indicated by a red traffic light or at a pedestrian crossing.

When the harness handle is lowered onto a guide dog's back it means the owner would appreciate assistance.

Always let a guide dog owner take your arm if he or she requires assistance – don't grab theirs.

The vast majority of the GDBA's guide dogs are bred by the Association.

The GDBA is involved in a wide range of activities, including organising holidays for clients, teaching braille to blind people, and veterinary research into guide dog health and pet bereavement. They also support work into the treatment and prevention of blindness in people.

The Association takes a great deal of care to match the right dog to the right owner. What are they trying to say to Sue Davis, then, by presenting her with Earl, a boisterous, affectionate Golden Retriever?

"I like to think I've got a good sense of humour," says Sue, "and I suppose I need it with Earl around. He was 15 months old when I got him and he wanted to investigate everything and take things out of the bin – he was very naughty.

"But Earl is also a very loving dog. He used to follow me everywhere and if I went out of the office for a short while he'd cry and whimper and really make quite a scene."

Earl sits behind Sue's desk each day at Lloyds Bank, where she works as a telephonist and audio typist. "He's very popular at the bank and keeps taking his rug to people as a present. Everyone makes a fuss of him."

But Earl had a hard act to follow when he joined Sue, for Inga, a Golden Retriever/Labrador cross had recently retired at the age of eleven. "We had some sulks to begin with," Sue admits, "but once Inga got uséd to Earl they started to play together and they're fine together now."

"The contrast between the two personalities is very obvious," Sue says. "My husband Justin and I took the pair of them on our honeymoon shortly after Earl came to live with us. Earl showed himself to be a real boy by sploshing and splashing in all the puddles while Inga walked sedately by my side. She's the lady and he's a real rascal!"

Gypsy

Gypsy meets a fundamental need for Gillian Batterham: she has completely changed Gillian's life and has opened the doors to a wide open world.

Gillian was born with retina pigmentatia, a condition she describes as being blinded by light. "Before I had Gypsy," Gillian told me, "I didn't go out anywhere on my own. I only went to the end of the street to catch the bus to work and then, at the end of the day, I'd come home again. I was a prisoner in my own home."

Before the Guide Dogs for the Blind Association would allow Gillian to have a dog, they told her she must practice walking with a long cane. "I hated it," said Gillian. "I felt very self conscious and I resolved to get it done as quickly as I could.

"Now I've got Gypsy, though, I don't care who knows. I've completely changed in the last year. We just love going out together and I'm proud to walk along the street with her."

Gillian says that Gypsy is a very friendly dog. "She loves it when people fuss her," says Gillian. "People talk to me when I'm out with her whereas before, even when I was out with my husband, they would speak to him instead of me because I couldn't see people smile or anything. I really felt left out because of it.

"Now people will pass the time of day with me and I've made a lot of new friends. I must say they speak to Gypsy before they speak to me because she's so gorgeous and she knows it!

"Gypsy is the best thing that's ever happened to me," she says. "We've never looked back. She loves her mum, too. The first time we met she came and sat beside me, and that's where she likes to be. At night I sit on the floor and she puts her head on my lap – I can't help but love her."

Dogs for disabled people

Janice Burns is a bubbling and vivacious qualified dental nurse, a wife, and the mother of two sons. At the age of 35, Janice was told that she suffered from a condition called syringomyelia which was compounded by a curvature of the spine, a prolapsed disk and a herniation of the brain.

The disease, which Janice describes as a cross between multiple sclerosis and motor neurone disease, effects her both neurologically and mechanically. Janice's body is so rigid that she is unable to bend, walking is difficult, and she is in constant pain.

Despite this," Janice told me, "it's important for me mentally and physically to keep as mobile as possible. I'm one of those people who is always looking for a solution, and I wasn't prepared to sit at home relying on my husband or elderly mother to pick something up for me when I dropped it."

Janice vaguely knew that there was an organisation which provided dogs to help disabled people, so she tracked them down. "I have never owned a dog," she says, "and I will admit to having been terrified of them."

46

Mark - 50th Dog for the Disabled

Janice made many phone calls, eventually discovering that a collaboration between Dogs for the Disabled and the Guide Dogs for the Blind Association would provide the solution.

Fletcher, a handsome Golden Retriever, had failed as a Guide Dog because he wouldn't accept his harness. As an assistance dog, however, Fletcher had the ideal personality.

"I am so disabled that I needed a dog that would be gentle, and I think it is this that made Dogs for the Disabled think Fletcher would be right for me. Even if you put a tissue paper on my leg it would hurt, but Fletcher is so soft and gentle he is just perfect."

Fletcher was trained up for his new role very quickly and was brought to Janice for a speedy introduction. "I had three days' training in the home. The trainer just brought Fletcher in and said, 'right, I'm going. I'll be back this evening.' I was literally thrown in at the deep end with no idea of what to do," Janice laughed.

"I lay down that afternoon and Fletcher just laid down beside me. I went to sleep and he went to sleep, and we just seemed to bond together. Now his place is by me in that same spot next to the settee."

Fletcher

49

Fletcher does everything Janice wants him to do. He picks up the television controller, fetches jumpers and skirts if she wants to get dressed, and retrieves items that have been dropped: "It's a matter of hot and cold," Janice explains. "I encourage him with my voice if he's going in the right direction.

"Fletcher enjoys working so much it's unbelievable. I really can't work him as hard as he would like, he just absolutely thrives on it. In fact, if I don't work him enough he makes sure I do because he picks everything up from everywhere and brings it to me!"

Fletcher's main problem seems to lie in his irresistibility. He is, according to Janice, a real show off. "He's just so incredibly attractive that people always stop to say hello. Everyone wants to stroke him and talk to him. We can't walk down the street but someone will stop us. But then, if they don't stop and say hello he gets quite disgusted, and I am really pleased that Fletcher has helped me to meet so many people."

And how has Janice's fear of dogs progressed? "I'm certainly not frightened of Fletcher, and the whole family is delighted that he has come to stay, he has fitted in so well. I can't describe the pleasure we experience when walking him – both my husband and I enjoy the walks which we simply didn't get before Fletcher joined the family."

48

Jackie Hodgkins with Olivia

47

Margaret Miles with Maggie

Hank's Harem

Hank lives with Roy and Pat Bartlett and eight beautiful Golden ladies. Lord of all he surveys, Hank is Top Dog at the Old Vicarage Kennels. "Hank looks after his bitches, that's for sure," says Pat Bartlett. He's not aggressive, but he certainly nudges his way in and asserts his position if anyone starts messing with his women."

Hank, son of Show Champion Westley Munro of Nortonwood, is rather special. He is Oliver's father, and Oliver, to steal a phrase, was a real chip off the old block. "Everyone loves Hank," Roy told me. We call him Nooky Bear because he looks just like a big teddy bear. He's full of fun but very very gentle."

The first time John and I met Hank, he was peering out through the front window of Roy and Pat's enormous ex-vicarage and issuing ferocious, belly-deep death threats. But once we were inside, Hank turned into a comedian. Hank is never happier than when he has a friendly human hand between his teeth and is dragging the body attached to the hand around the room.

50

Daisey & Hank - (Abnalls Jolly Roger - Sh. Ch. Westley Munro of Nortonwood ex Davern Jollity)

51

The Tiarpica Ladies

44

Tammie was Hank's first wife. "You couldn't wish for a dog with a better temperament," says Pat, "she was just brilliant. She loved being mated and having her puppies. She used to prance around as if to say, 'look at me, I'm going to have puppies'. Even if puppies came onto the television, Tammie was there, trying to get at them. She just loved everything in life; she could accept absolutely everything.

"Tammie had three major operations but she never ever cried or complained. If she was a person, she would be the sort of person you look at and think, 'isn't she lovely'. She had peace of mind, and if you've got that you've got everything."

The beautiful Krystal is another perfect mother. Besotted by her two grown-up daughters, Bo and Charlotte, Krystal spends her evenings fussing over them, playing and keeping them clean. Bo and Charlotte are both as soft as each other. They are such pretty little ladies, racing each other to the nearest available lap, cuddling and kissing, and soaking up all the attention. A perfect antidote to any broken heart.

Jazz is another of Krystal's progeny. The first time we met, Jazz was crawling along on the floor on her belly. "Jazz had been living in a home with very small dogs," says Pat. "She was there for fourteen months but came back to me because I was told she was vicious towards the other dogs.

"When she first came back she was like a thalidomide dog, as if she had no legs to stand on. She seemed absolutely petrified. We introduced her gradually to our family, and yet we couldn't find anything vicious about her at all. She's absolutely fine now, part of the family, and very very happy. I don't know why she had the problem, we will never know; but I often wonder whether her exuberant personality was frowned upon and she tried to be smaller, like the others, to gain approval."

Candy, another of Hank's beautiful wives, is the pack leader. "If we wanted to leave something down in the room, Candy would make sure none of the others touched it," said Roy. "Yet nobody would realise she's the boss because she's so quiet and unassuming."

Penny was a rescue bitch who was very disturbed when Roy and Pat first met her. "During her first night with us she caused about £400 worth of damage," says Pat. "She tore velvet curtains to pieces, ate the carpet and the underlay, and even made a dent in the concrete floor. Despite that, she was very beautiful and I could see that her behaviour had a lot to do with the way she had been treated."

Today, Penny is a caring mother and the only Golden Roy and Pat know who can keep her toys for years without chewing them up. There are absolutely no clues which would point the most determined detective towards her earlier unruly behaviour.

"It is tempting for a breeder to hold the owner responsible for any problems a puppy might have," says Pat. "But that is not always the case. Breeders need to know what is happening with the puppies they produce so that they can ensure they are not enforcing any bad traits in subsequent litters.

"Occasionally, though, you do find a Golden in the wrong environment and behavioural problems can arise. You need to be sensible and examine the situation – it doesn't necessarily mean it's a bad dog. Just like children, Goldens need tender loving care, and the occasional respite from a life of boredom."

Lastly, but certainly not least, there is Daisy. "Daisy is the real character in the family," says Roy. "We sometimes sit and laugh at her rather than watch television – she is such a hoot. She's the sort of dog you just have to look at to feel happy inside; she has 'comedian' written all over her." (Roy and Pat daren't leave Daisy in a room alone with my husband, for they know that John has avaricious intentions.)

So this is Hank's Harem. No wonder he's such a happy boy!

Little Bo died suddenly under anaesthetic; Tammie completed her mission before publication at a great old age. Both are sadly missed.

Canine Partners for Independence

Golden Retrievers, with their intelligent yet sensitive natures, have been found to be the ideal dogs for people who need a helping hand. Canine Partners for Independence (CPI), a British charity which trains dogs to help people with disabilities, uses only Golden Retrievers – and these Retrievers are very carefully bred to bring their caring personalities to the fore.

Training purpose bred dogs to assist people with physical disabilities was first developed by Canine Companions for Independence (CCI) in the USA. The first programme to be established in Europe, the SOHO Foundation, was pioneered at a nursing home in Nijmegen in 1984, and the American CCI helped SOHO to train its first instructor, who spent a year working in America studying CCI's selection and training techniques for both dogs and recipients.

SOHO uses mainly Golden Retrievers, acquired as puppies from qualified breeders in the UK, and it was to SOHO that the UK's CPI turned to obtain initial training for the charity's first instructor. How's that for co-operation?

Canine Partners for Independence are very highly trained dogs – reacting to some 96 commands. They can reach up to open and close doors, turn light switches on and off, and press lift buttons. They pick up dropped items and retrieve out-of-reach objects from table tops, shelves and counters.

They understand the names of many different articles which they can fetch on command. They understand the words for where to place the items – such as table, shelf or counter – or they will place items in the owner's hands if requested. They will also pass items to another person, such as a cashier when out shopping.

Mrs Anne Conway, the founder of CPI, says, "Recipients are carefully selected; training is thorough; and each project needs a sound financial basis.

"Dogs must be both physically and temperamentally suited to the work and they must be acceptable to the general public. The Golden Retriever is a very suitable breed due to its gentle, biddable temperament, and friendliness towards people and other animals."

CPI contends that both genetics and environment play an important part in the physical and mental development of dogs. "Since puppies start reacting to the world around them while still in the nest," says Mrs Conway, "anything they learn from then onwards will affect their future temperament and working ability. A highly selective breeding programme, with optimum rearing and training conditions, ensures the best possible results."

Of equal importance is the selection and training of the recipients. "They must be willing to give the dog proper care and attention," says Anne Conway. "They must be willing to attend an intensive residential training course, and the home and surrounding environment must also be suitable."

The most common disabilities likely to benefit from an assistance dog are:

Cerebral Palsy
Osteoarthritis
Multiple Sclerosis
Rheumatoid Arthritis
Parkinson's Disease
Spinal Injuries
Spina Bifida
Polio
Friedrich's Ataxia
Paget's Disease

Training of human recipients is thorough: people must plumb their innermost depths to move from disability to ability; from dependence to independence. As well as learning the 96 commands the dogs already understand, recipients attend lectures in many subjects, including dog psychology and motivation, dog handling and obedience skills, dog care and management, preventative veterinary care, and other related topics.

They also receive assertiveness training so that they can work in partnership with their dogs. The course ends with theoretical and practical tests. Following graduation, the recipient returns home with the dog, and there is considerable and careful follow-up by the instructors for the rest of the dog's life.

As Anne Conway points out, most of us take our physical health for granted. "But for someone with severe mobility problems," she says, "everyday life can prove to be a series of frustrating obstacles. Even with a constant carer in attendance and the best facilities available, many people are virtually housebound or tied to an institution.

The partnership between human and canine partner means that disability is replaced by greater ability; lack of confidence is replaced by increased confidence; frustration is replaced by motivation; lack of responsibility is replaced by responsibility for the dog; the feeling of conspicuousness is replaced by the dog as a focal point; the lack of understanding is replaced by sharing with the dog; the denial of the condition is replaced by a willingness to discuss it; and lack of opportunity is replaced by an increase in opportunity."

The Joke and Falco Partnership

Joke Schröder has shared her life with Falco the Golden Retriever for over four years. Born with a muscular disease which deteriorates with time, Joke uses a wheelchair and has very little power in her arms. "I love animals," Joke says, "but I thought I couldn't have a dog. It would have been very difficult for me to train a dog because I would find it impossible to make him understand I am the boss. Then I heard about SOHO from a friend, and after some serious training he came to live with me.

"In the beginning it was so difficult for Falco to do things for me because I was his third boss – first the puppy walker, then the trainer, then me. There was also so much for me to learn. The dog has to like you, and you have to do it the right way and learn dog psychology.

"I spent two weeks at the SOHO training camp where they introduced me to a number of dogs and then set out to decide which was suitable for me – they knew the dogs all right, but they didn't know me that well, so they had to find the best combination.

"The course was very interesting, although it was hard work. They taught us how dogs think and how to establish dominance: the good ways to tell a dog things. We were especially taught how to praise."

What does Falco do for Joke? "He opens doors: pulls the handle down with his leg and pushes it outwards. If he needs to close a door he pulls a rope. He puts his nose on a button to move the elevator."

How does he know which floor Joke wants to go to?

"He knows that if we are going down I give a command for a low floor. If we are going up, he is told to jump. If he doesn't jump high enough, I ask him to jump higher."

Falco will also give Joke's purse to assistants in shops. If he wants to go in the garden he opens the door, goes to the toilet, and lets himself back in!

Joke works as a telephone operator and it is imperative that none of her colleagues unwittingly spoil Falco's training. "The main thing is that nobody touches him," says Joke. "Even if people come to my house they must not touch him – I have to be the main person in his life, and other people are able to seduce him very easily."

Joke and Falco

52

The training has been successful: the bond is strong. "Falco panics if he can't accompany me everywhere," says Joke. He's such a happy boy who loves it when he's allowed to play the clown. He particularly likes it when I send him off to fetch something – he charges around the house having a great time.

"Falco has changed my life," Joke concludes. "The total rhythm is so different now. I go outside in the street and people are not looking at me but at the dog. We talk a lot to other people who have dogs. And I'm responsible for a living being."

Cinderella and the
Happy Ending

Purbarn Cinderella won her first field trial certificate of merit when she was 16 months old. From that day on at shows, Cindy was placed (first, second, third, fourth or fifth) every time she entered a field trial class. She has won the Heydown Perpetual Cup for best of sex; the Patiala Cup at the GRC Championship Show, and the Deustraw Cup, twice. Cindy's crowning glory was to win the coveted Gold Challenge Trophy at Crufts in 1987.

Now nearly thirteen years old, Cindy's main joy in life is dinner time, for when food is about she dances around and tries to act like a puppy, literally barking with glee. Cindy has earned herself a place at the centre of the family: she is very faithful, she's a big softie, and she still insists upon accompanying her owner, Jenny Frankland-Burton, out in the field.

"Last season she was only allowed to help for two days," says Jenny. "Next season, much to her disgust, she will have to stay at home and let her great great grandson Razz, and great great great granddaughter Purdy do the work instead.

Jenny says that Cindy is terribly eager to work – so much so that she was quite prepared to go on a shoot whilst she still bore the stitches from her hysterectomy. Needless to say, she was quite put out when Jenny left her behind. But the very day after she had her stitches out, Cindy insisted upon doing a full day's work. "She's a remarkable old lady who has always done everything she could to please me," says Jenny. "She still would do – if only I would let her. Sadly, in Cindy's case the mind is willing but the body is no longer quite so good."

The events leading up to Cinderella's Gold Trophy victory required endurance, too.

One of Jenny's bitches, Cheeta, had a 'blank' season which meant that there was no physical evidence to show that she was ready for mating. Another bitch, Fee, was due to be mated on the Monday the very day Jenny discovered another favourite, Thunder, acting the macho stud dog with Cheeta.

That particular evening it was pouring with rain, and Jenny had arranged to take Fee off to the stud dog – after she had milked the goat and let all the bitches into the garden for a run. "Then I put the goat away, brought Fee, who was in season, into the house, and let the dogs out," says Jenny. "Thunder went straight up to Cheeta and mounted her."

Jenny told Thunder that he had it all wrong, that Cheeta was not in season. But Thunder knew better, and Jenny spent half an hour in the pouring rain with Thunder and Cheeta tied to one-another before going back to the house dripping wet to phone the stud dog owner to say they would be late.

Three weeks later, Jenny took Fee and Cheeta to the vet. He agreed that Cheeta wasn't in whelp, but that Fee was, but ten days before the puppies were due, Jenny and her vet agreed they had been wrong.

"Both Fee and Cheeta were due to whelp on the Monday, and the Thursday before that my father had a heart attack," says Jenny. "I arranged for a friend to look after the children and set off for the hospital, took my mother home, fed her, and then drove back to my own house.

"When I arrived, my friend asked me when the bitches were due, because Fee had been rushing around in circles all evening and going in and out of the whelping box scratching up paper. Fee looked at me as if to say, 'Thank goodness you're home mum, now I can get on with it'. Half an hour later we had the first puppy. We ended up with nine, and Fee and I looked after them in between visits to the hospital. We lost one fading puppy on the Sunday, but the others were fine.

"On the Monday my father had a turn for the worse, so it was a mad panic rush to the hospital. I picked up my mother and dropped the kids off at the ex mother in-law's, took mum to the hospital, took her home, fed her, and went back to my house to find Cheeta running around in circles saying, 'I don't know what to do, I'm in labour and I've never done it before. Oh heck, what do I do now?'."

The Purban Kennels - (left to right) Purdy, Fee, Razz, Kizzie, Maya, Thunder & Cindy (lying down)

Half an hour later Cheeta had her first puppy, and she too had nine. So that was 17 puppies within four days of each other plus Jenny's father in hospital. Both litters had their fair share of escape artists so Jenny put all the escape artists into one bed with high sides, and all the others into the other one, and both bitches would feed either lot. Jenny could tell them apart, even if no-one else could!

The following week was Crufts and, despite the exhaustion, Jenny set off with Cindy . Much to her delight, Cindy won the field trial class, shortly after which Jenny dashed off to ring the hospital to find out how her father was, and also her friend who was looking after the puppies. When she got back, the girl on the next bench told her that Joan Gill had shown Cindy for her.

Jenny exclaimed that she had shown Cindy herself!. The girl explained that Cindy had earned a place in the Challenge for the Gold Trophy, but Jenny, dropping from exhaustion, knew nothing of any Gold Trophy.

"Well I charged up to Joan and asked her, 'What's this about you showing Cindy for me?'. Joan said 'I hope you don't mind Jenny, but we couldn't find you anywhere. I showed her in the Challenge for you. She won, so don't worry about it.'

"I was absolutely flabbergasted, but of course, over the moon. The following day I was able to go off to the hospital, trophy in arms, to show my father. He was absolutely thrilled, but I was totally exhausted. I swore never to have two litters so close together again."

The Trophy took place of honour in the house for a year, and Cindy basked in the glory. All 17 puppies grew up strong and healthy, dad made a slow recovery – and Jenny somehow managed to avoid having a nervous breakdown!

Jamie

The people's friend

PAT Dogs give institutions a feeling of homeliness and normality; they add interest and distraction to the day's routine; they provide unconditional, non-judgmental love and affection, and they offer patients a substitute for their own dear missed pets. An analysis of the first 2,200 registered PAT dogs shows that Golden Retrievers are number one, followed by Labradors, German Shepherds, Cavalier King Charles Spaniels and then Border Collies.

Jamie is a friendly, sociable and good natured registered PAT Dog who has extended his realm of operation to become a co-therapist with his owners. Dorothy Cyster is a Nurse Tutor for Care of the Dying. So impressed with the benefits pets have brought to patients and carers, Dorothy now works in a voluntary capacity as PAT Dogs co-ordinator for Gloucestershire.

"Bringing Jamie into teaching sessions," says Dorothy, "has heightened nurses' awareness of the benefits of pet therapy. Jamie's support has also been incalculable in my professional role as a nurse tutor for the care of the dying."

"Jamie can put anxious students at their ease and he helps to 'warm up' a newly formed class. Many students naturally find it difficult to discuss personal feelings and fears in relation to death, but stroking Jamie or even watching him sleep peacefully

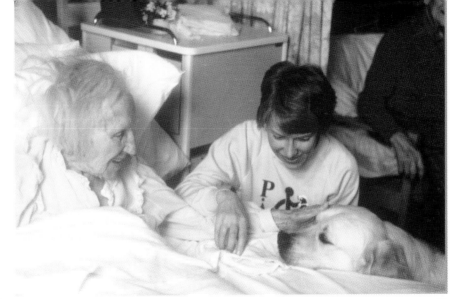

54

Jamie on duty

beside me has a reassuring effect. Jamie is also an asset in communication skills training as he is able to demonstrate non-verbal communication.

Dorothy also feels that teaching staff appear to benefit from Jamie's presence. They often comment that he alleviates stress by providing distraction from the day's problems. One newly-appointed tutor told Dorothy that when Jamie greeted her on her first day at the College, she immediately felt at ease and knew that she had come to a friendly place of work.

Jamie is also a welcomed visitor at St Michael's Hospice, Hereford, and the Sue Ryder Home in Cheltenham. He provides immense comfort to grieving relatives, and attends the Bereavement Support Group at Delancey Hospital on a regular basis.

"Many people are too upset to speak when they have lost a loved one," says Dorothy, "but Jamie nuzzles in beside them, puts his head on their knees, and looks up at them with his big soulful eyes. He seems to understand and offers comfort. You really have to witness these encounters to appreciate the strength of the interaction."

Perhaps Jamie is a reincarnation of a loving saint, for he also offers support to Dorothy's husband Richard, who counsels at the local Alcohol Counselling and Information Service. "People who suffer from drinking problems often have a very low self-esteem," Richard told me. "Jamie is not judgmental, but welcomes them. He transcends all the difficulties of human interaction. With stressful clients he can calm them down after counselling and lighten the situation, and where couples find difficulty in communicating, he can encourage them to speak to him."

Dorothy says that when off duty, Jamie needs his relaxation. "He enjoys chasing anything that moves," she says. "He is a naughty puppy at times but still a big sop!"

The bond

Mrs Marianne Mays represents a perfect example of the two-way bond which can grow between human beings and their Goldens, and she illustrates the painful choices which need to be made when considering whether a dog should be kept in quarantine when entering the British Isles. Marianne, who is Swedish by birth, lives with her husband Nick in Yorkshire.

Marianne and Nick are real animal lovers, with four dogs, nine cats, and hundreds of rabbits, hamsters and mice. They show and breed the smaller animals and cats, but the dogs are mainly pets.

Jesper

Marianne acquired her first Golden Retriever, Master, in 1981, when she was living in Sweden. "It wasn't really planned," she says. "I just started walking him in the afternoons as his owners worked during the day. Eventually they decided to re-home him and offered him to me."

When Marianne lost Master, she felt that she needed another Golden as soon as possible as she had become completely hooked on the breed. "That is how Jesper came into my life," she said. Jesper was born on the day that Master died. "Very early on," says Marianne, "a very strong bond developed between us."

At only nine-and-a-half weeks old, Jesper was taken seriously ill with a bad stomach upset and he was kept at the vet's for four days on an intravenous drip. Thankfully, Jesper came home, and soon after Marianne took him to obedience classes. "He was very quick to learn, and we both enjoyed it," Marianne explains. "He could walk to heel to a very high standard when he was only 16 weeks old. We received much praise for the fact that Jesper was so very attached to me despite his tender age."

Jesper was a very small Golden, having lost a lot of weight when he was ill. In fact, at puppy training classes he was usually selected to play with the small breeds such as Dachshunds rather than the other Goldens. At 16 weeks of age the illness struck again, and he was back at the vet's on a drip once again.

"No-one could say what was wrong," Marianne recalls. "I received lots of advice from friends and vets and they all told me to have Jesper put to sleep as he was so sickly and would never grow to be a 'proper dog'. I refused and brought him home again. He was thin, but happy."

Marianne began to experiment with Jesper's diet and soon realised that he was completely incapable of taking any dog food or meat. Fish didn't work either. Everything seemed to give him terrible stomach upsets with vomiting and diarrhoea. "In the end I found a diet that suited him fine, although it did seem to be a strange one, consisting of cooked rice, white bread and pancakes plus extra vitamins and calcium."

When Jesper was four years old, Marianne moved to England to marry Nick. "At first I told my husband-to-be that there was no way I would leave Sweden without Jesper, but I thought long and hard and decided that he would be happier if I left him at home in familiar surroundings, without the need to go into quarantine for six months. He had never been fond of new places, and he hadn't spent a day of his life in kennels. I felt it would be fairer to leave him with my mother where he had lived all his life."

55

Marianne missed Jesper terribly, even asking her mother to hold the phone to his ear so that she could speak to him from time to time. But although Marianne's mother didn't want to worry her, Jesper's personality was changing. He began to lose weight and developed cysts between his toes which sometimes prevented him from walking. He developed an ear infection and wouldn't come when called any more. And he became very nervous, refusing to go for walks with anyone but Marianne's mother or brother.

"A neighbour used to take him for long walks," says Marianne, "but that had to stop as Jesper wouldn't go with him. He even started to dislike going away on holiday to my mother's house in the country – but he had loved those holidays before. All in all he sounded like a very unhappy dog."

Nick suggested to Marianne that perhaps Jasper was unhappy because he missed her. Worried, Marianne went to Sweden to visit Jesper – where she received a deliriously happy reception. "My mother said that she hadn't seen him so happy since I left," Marianne confirms. "He remembered everything I had ever taught him and was once again my very happy dog, although he was very ill."

Marianne soon discovered that Jesper didn't come when called because he was almost deaf – the constant infections had caused the ear canals to grow together. Luckily, Marianne had taught Jesper a sort of sign language as a puppy so she was able to communicate with him without any problems.

"The decision was easy," says Marianne. "He had to come and live with us in England." And so Jesper was put into quarantine for six long months. Marianne visited three to five times a week: "The staff at the kennels were wonderful, and Jesper didn't seem to mind being there."

The six months eventually passed and Jesper was released from quarantine in June 1990, and introduced to Leo, Marianne's English Golden Retriever, and Bonnie a Cocker Spaniel bitch. "It took a while for Jesper to settle in with Leo," she says, "but once they had established that Leo, although younger, was top dog, there were no problems and the two Goldens became very firm friends."

Jesper is now a very different dog to the one Marianne brought home from Sweden. His ears have been operated on but to no avail: he is still deaf and suffers from ear infections. The interdigital cysts have disappeared altogether and Jesper has put on weight, and for the first time in his life he is able to eat meat without any stomach problems. "He is a truly happy dog," Marianne concludes.

"Jesper is very friendly and gentle. He loves all dogs and all people, and other animals too. He is well behaved – in fact, Jesper is an absolute joy to own."

Indian children were taught from the beginning to love and respect all creatures and all forms of life, and as a result animals responded readily to the light of love in their hearts.

White Eagle in 'Sun Men of the Americas' by Grace Cooke.

Thirty thousand miles in pursuit of excellence

John says that he would quite like to come back as a Golden Retriever in his next life. I have one proviso: were I to do the same, I'd like to live with someone like Lyn Anderson who breathes freedom into the Linchael kennels.

Linchael Goldens, all eighteen of them, have the run of the house, the run of the farm, the run of the barns, and the run of the cow sheds. "The farmhouse door is open all the time," says Lyn. "The dogs tend to come and go and do jobs with my husband. They help to feed the cows and generally get in the way, but they thoroughly enjoy themselves.

"It's ideal for a Golden really, because they are busy all day. Even if they're digging holes they're busy. They like to play where we store the straw for the cattle, and they love chasing mice. They are never bored or unattended, which I think is so important. Goldens rate human company above all else."

Not only are the Linchael Goldens happy, but they're also incredibly beautiful. "The dynasty began," says Lyn, "with Anna, known formally as Rossbourne Angelene. Anna is responsible for many many champions through her grandchildren.

"She was, I suppose, the greatest character of all time. If Anna felt she was being ignored for any length of time during the evenings, she would suddenly rush to the front door barking furiously. My husband would get up to see who was there and of course, he would always seem to miss the end of a thrilling film, and I would lose my place in my book. By the time we opened the door, Anna was lying back asleep again but grinning from ear to ear.

"It was just a ploy to get us to our feet, and it worked without fail over a period of about twelve years. There was always the possibility that someone was really there."

Anna's daughter is the acclaimed Show Champion Linchael Delmoss, who has produced eight title-holding children in the UK and abroad, with several more in the making. Delmoss is the supreme mother, even taking over the task of nurturing when her daughter, Linchael Wild Cherry, tragically died at the age of three, leaving a litter of six-week old pups behind.

"I had a dreadful feeling that the pups knew their mother had gone," says Lyn, "but Delmoss moved in and cleaned them up. We have a bitch to this day who thinks that Delmoss is her mother, and Delmoss is absolutely convinced that she's her puppy. She washes her bottom and her ears, and licks round her mouth and eyes in a very maternal way."

In addition to looking after eighteen Goldens, showing them, and teaching full time, Lyn goes to evening classes with whichever of her dogs needs practice with basic obedience before working in the field. "At the moment it's Percy at obedience," says Lyn, "and he's just the clown of the class, providing endless amusement for everyone there. A few weeks ago the trainer told me to stop laughing when Percy was running towards me, so I suggested she come and stand behind me, see what I was seeing, and try to keep a straight face herself.

"When Percy is on a recall he folds his ears back behind his head and curls his mouth into a great wide grin. You can see his whole set of teeth, top and bottom. The idea is for the handler to remain absolutely motionless, without any display of emotion when the dog's working. Nevertheless, there was a great shriek from the trainer behind – she found Percy as funny as I did."

Lyn and her aristocratic Goldens are to be seen at virtually every show in the country, travelling, on average, about 30,000 miles each year. Why? Lyn supposes it's the absolute quest for perfection.

Lyn is surprised when anyone says they don't go to shows to win, because it is such a dreadfully expensive hobby. "It becomes a way of life," she says. "But after you've been showing for a while you don't mind so much if you are beaten. There are all sorts of reasons why you don't win. There are other good dogs, and I don't doubt that personalities must sometimes enter into the decision.

"Sometimes, though, it does you good to eat a little humble pie, although I mind very much if I have to eat humble pie after travelling thousands of miles to get there!"

Having started with her Goldens in 1965, Lyn has a great deal of experience under her belt. Does she have any tips for the aspiring exhibitor?

"Spend some time looking first," she says. "Go and sit at the ring side and watch how it happens. Then I think it's extremely important to go to a ringcraft class. I've just come back from Denmark where, like most European countries now, the entry fee per class has gone up to over £20 – a lot of money. Just over a quarter of my entry wasn't ring trained at all. The owners stood there, the dogs played, and in one case the dog rolled.

"It's very difficult for a judge to assess a dog when it's upside down or generally playing about. Go to ringcraft classes: they're great fun, great for socialising the dog, and they are very good for the owner who wants to find out what happens at a show."

Lyn is very adamant that when showing ceases to be fun it's time to call it a day. Dogs are just like people and some enjoy showing and others don't. You get total extroverts and you get the quieter ones. One of Lyn's extroverts, Linchael Gullviva, must kiss a hundred people before she goes home. Rosie, as she is called, was one of the year's really top winners in her age group. She has a presence that you could never put there.

Lyn says that you can tell whether a dog has charisma at around twelve weeks old when ring training starts. "I can sum them up when I'm grooming them, I can just feel it. People come to be kissed by Rosie: she spends her time out of the ring climbing on every lap and kissing every person. She's a terrific show off and it does help.

"However, because the competition is so high, you need to have looks as well as personality."

Meanwhile, back at the farm, the Linchael Goldens are settling down for a good night's sleep. Once again, it's an open house policy. All eighteen wander around the house at night, and the doors are open. Some like to lie in the cool hall, one is rather partial to the bathroom, others sleep by Lyn's bed. "Some prefer to sleep outside," says Lyn. "But then, it's a very short night anyway. My husband is up before six to tend to the cows, and off we all go again."

56

busy, busy, busy - Lyn and friends at home

The Pilgrimage

I went on a pilgrimage to visit Ron and Madge Bradbury, owners of the respected Nortonwood Golden Retrievers. The late Champion Nortonwood Faunus won 13 Challenge Certificates in his day, and he was a prolific sire. He was the top stud dog in the breed for eight years running, and 'Dog World's' top gun dog stud in the UK in 1985. In 1986 Faunus became top stud dog of all breeds, with a record number of points – and he's yet to be equalled.

Faunus was the father of Show Champion Westley Munro of Nortonwood. Westley Munro of Nortonwood was the father of Abnalls Jolly Roger, known as Hank. Hank was the father of Oliver, my Oliver. Oliver was handsome and intelligent, and he had a beautiful temperament – just like his Father, Grandfather, and his Great-Grandfather.

58

Ch. Nortonwood Faunus (Ch. Camrose Cabus Christopher ex Nortonwood Fantasy of Milo)

I wonder if the Bradburys appreciate the happiness they have brought to so many human beings through the Nortonwood line?

When I arrived at the Bradbury's home, Show Champion Nortonwood Silvanus and his son, Show Champion Jobeka Jasper of Nortonwood, came to greet me. Silvanus, known affectionately as Simba, took my hand in his great soft mouth, and Jasper proudly showed me his beautiful cushion. Jasper sang: "woo woo myom woo myom," and the two big boys clambered onto my lap, my hand still held gently by the eight year-old Simba

It was a welcome fit for a Queen, and I was cuddled and caressed until the visit was over.

We snuggled down and watched a video showing many of the Nortonwood beauties, past and present. Alert expressions, happy smiling eyes, waggy tails, shimmering coats, and keen intelligence paraded on the screen in front of me. It was doggie heaven. Jasper was appreciative, too, and thought it was great fun to watch his Golden relatives on the television screen.

Ron and Madge Bradbury acquired their first Golden Retriever in the late 1950s and, of course, the Golden Bug bit. Having bred many champion dogs and, being respected show judges the world over, Mr and Mrs Bradbury say that their Golden friends have opened up the world for them: Italy, Israel, Norway, Sweden, Finland, Holland, Belgium, Switzerland, Spain, Zimbabwe, Germany, Barbados, Argentina – in search of the perfect Golden.

57

Roo - (Sh. Ch. Westley Munro of Nortonwood - Ch. Nortonwood Faunus ex Ch. Westley Victoria)

We played with Dilly, the Bradbury's up-and-coming youngster: Jasper's 16-week-old pup. Such a pretty little girl, and so full of fun. Like her father, Dilly is rather partial to cushions – it's interesting to see how these proclivities pass through lines.

To the Bradburys, temperament is vital. "Faunus was a gentle dog," Madge Bradbury told me. "He didn't have a nasty streak in him. He particularly loved children and enjoyed playing with them."

At one time Ron and Madge Bradbury had five stud dogs living in the house together. "We never had a bad word," Ron told me. "Their temperaments were lovely."

Show Champion Westley Munro of Nortonwood was a very intelligent dog who was, quite literally, full of bounce. "Munro acquired the pet name of Rue," said Madge, "because he was always jumping about like a baby kangaroo. He used to jump over our five-barred gate just to go and meet people.

"Rue also had rather a penchant for balls – but it couldn't be any old ball, it had to be a special one. We used to take him to the toy stalls at the dog shows and he would rummage around in the boxes until he found the very ball he was looking for. Even if we picked out what we thought was the best one, Rue would carry on looking until the perfect ball surfaced. Well, he had won best of breed, so he was entitled to pick his own!"

And now young Jasper, Simba's son, is also a toy boy: "When we had little puppies here recently," said Ron, "Jasper would go out into the garden to play. He used to leap right over the puppies, pinch one of their toys, and then run round the garden with it.

"No," said Ron, "once you've had a Golden Retriever, you wouldn't want to be without one again."

Certainly not if it's a bouncy, flouncy, funny, happy, jolly, handsome, huggable Golden Retriever!

Mrs and Mrs R. Bradbury with the current Nortonwood family

59

57

Golden Retrievers –

As Champion Sinnhein Sebastian's owner John Clarke points out, there are many good things to have come from Scotland, and Golden Retrievers are one of the best!

The beautiful Golden Rhurie lives with Jim Stafford and his wife Mary, only a stone's throw away from the birthplace of Robert Burns, Scotland's most famous poet. Rhurie is a proud young fellow, no doubt fully aware of his aristocratic heritage, and intending one day to put his name on the list of 'better Scottish champions'.

It was Sir Dudley Marjoriebanks, known later as the first Lord Tweedmouth, who created the Golden Retriever in his search for the perfect hunting dog. From the Guisachan country estate, which nestled amidst the picturesque Scottish Highlands, Lord Tweedmouth mated Nous, a yellow Wavy-coated Retriever, with Belle, a Tweed Water Spaniel. Two bitches, Cowslip and Primrose, were retained from the first litter. Cowslip was mated to Tweed, a second Tweed Water Spaniel, and from this union came Topsy.

Topsy was mated to Sambo, who is thought to be a black Flat-coated Retriever or Wavy-coated Retriever. Interestingly, Flat-coated Retrievers had been 'created' in England from crosses between the St. John's Newfoundland (not the Newfoundland we recognise today) and Setters.

Anyway, Cowslip was again mated, this time to Sampson, an Irish Setter. For more than twenty years, Lord Tweedmouth carefully linebred back to Cowslip, and it is also thought that a sandy-coloured Bloodhound was used. The result was the Ilchester line of Goldens – the ancestors of all Goldens today. God bless Lord Tweedmouth.

Sadly, having contacted a few of Lord Tweedmouth's descendants to see if there was a continuity today, I discovered that none of the family now keeps Goldens.

Now, getting back to Rhurie . . . Rhurie was born in Birmingham, 300 long miles away from his new home in Scotland. Rhurie's mother Chloe had been taken to Scotland for the mating with Sebastian, and she delivered her beautiful brood back at home in the British Midlands.

It was when Jim Stafford saw Sebastian – best of breed at Crufts 1990 – on the television advertising a well-known brand of dog food, that he said: "If ever I have another Golden, I'll have one like that. Sebastian is the ultimate in Golden Retrievers."

His family took Jim at his word, making a 600-mile round trip to present seven-week old Rhurie to him during his 50th birthday celebrations. His daughter Morag began the quest by writing to Pedigree Petfoods to find John Clarke, Sebastian's breeder, who told Morag about John Seymour down in Birmingham. The birthday party was arranged, and Jim Jnr. and his wife Audrey made an excuse so that they could be late for the party without arousing suspicion, before setting off to collect the pup.

"I could have cried," said Jim Snr. when Rhurie arrived. "The puppy was so beautiful. When they told me who his father was, I was totally gobsmacked! Words couldn't express it."

And so it is that Rhurie, the beautiful Golden Retriever, has returned home to Scotland, the Motherland, the land of his forefathers.

A Golden Family Tradition

The Earl of Northesk told me that some time before the First World War, his father bought a Golden Retriever dog called Glory, which was surprising as he was never very good with dogs and they never particularly liked him. Soon after, the late Earl rejoined his regiment, so Glory was left with the current Earl's grandmother, the Hon. Mrs Douglas Carnegie. "My grandmother," said Lord Northesk, "had an affinity with all animals and she was especially good with dogs."

It was with Glory in 1916 that the Heydown Golden Retrievers began, a kennel that is remembered as one of the 'great' dual purpose kennels of all time. 'Heydown' was a part Queen Ann family house that was extensively altered in 1840, and renamed Fair Oak, and it was from this that the kennel took its name. Mrs

61

The Earl of Northesk with Dee and Dum

Carnegie and Mrs Charlesworth, who founded the famous Noranby kennel in 1906 with a bitch called Normanby Beauty, were two of the leading Golden Retriever trainers and breeders between the wars.

"As a child," said Lord Northesk, "I can remember the pack. At times my grandmother had a considerable number and every afternoon, come rain or sun, she and my aunt could be seen exercising anything up to twenty dogs, and at the same time working with some of them. They were always marvelously gentle and tolerant with children, and never objected to being sat upon or pulled about. Despite their high degree of training, because most of them were bred for work as well as the bench, my grandmother usually allowed and even encouraged the older and more experienced to play.

"In the summer we all used to swim together in the river Rother which ran through the estate. It was only mildly hazardous in as much as the dogs used to inadvertently duck you from time to time – but I am sure that if I really got into trouble, they would have retrieved me."

Lord Northesk remembers some individuals, particularly Heydown Guider as he was allowed into the house once he retired. He was a big red-coloured dog who was Field Trial Champion three times and a Show Champion as well. "I also remember Field Trial Champion Heydown Guillieflower who was a pale coloured bitch, and the other two famous dogs were Gunner and Grip, both Field Trial Champions, although both of these were a bit before my time."

The Heydown kennel came to an end when Mrs Carnegie died in 1952, and it wasn't until 1957 that Lord Northesk acquired a Golden Retriever for himself. Sharland Swagger was bred by Joyce Munday from the Heydown strain (Ms Munday's kennel name was Sharland). "Swagger was a fairly pale coloured bitch with tremendous courage," says the Earl. "She was marvelously biddable and very easy to train. Like all my Goldens she was wonderful with the children."

60

Twit

Golden Retriever Foundation Pedigree

Ch. Heydown Gunner (1921)	*Glory of Fyning (1916)*	Normanby Balfour (1911)	Culham Brass (1904)	Dust (1901)
				Chlores
			Normanby Beauty (1906)	unknown
				unknown
		Stella of Fyning (1914)	Astley Storm (1912)	Culham Coffee
				Paddiford Duchess
			Griff (1910)	Proud Ben (1909)
				Red Queen (1905)
-also - Ch. Heydown Grip and Heydown Gurth	*Stagden Cross Pamela (1920)*	Prior (1913)	Paxhill Brian (1911)	Crane Point (Scamp)
				Inez (by Rajah)
			Culham Bronze (1908)	Culham Brass
				Culham Rossa (1903)
		Stagden Cross Honey (1919)	Ingestre Ben (1915)	Ingestre Bunty (1915)
				Toptwig
			Rossa	Klip (1911)
				Ingestre Rubina
Onaway (1922)	*Ch. & FT Ch. Balcombe Boy (1919)*	Culham Tip (1913)	Culham Copper (1908)	Culham Brass (1904)
				Culham Rossa (1903)
			Beena (1911)	Ingestre Scamp (1906)
				Ingestre Tyne (1905)
		Culham Amber II	unknown	unknown
				unknown
			unknown	unknown
				unknown
also Haulstone Dan, Amber Dimple, Balcombe Pride and Haulstone Rusty	*Balcombe Bunty*	Ottershaw Brilliant (1919)	Ottershaw Sovereign	Ch. Noranby Campfire (1912)
				Ballingdon Floss (1914)
			Ottershaw Blush	unknown
				unknown
		Syrup (1919)	Culham Tip (1913)	Culham Copper (1908)
				Beena (1911)
			Honey	unknown
				unknown

Pedigree of Ch. Cubbington Diver and Cubbington Fion. - Born October, 1924

Bred by - Capt. Escombe
Cubbington Diver was owned by Mrs Cottingham
Cubbington Fion was owned by Mrs Morgan

Lord Northesk began to believe that Swagger could count, because at the end of a very big day of picking up at Cowdray Park, Sussex, the Earl asked a young man to try to drop his pheasants in front of a mass of tangled rhododendrons rather than put the tired dog to extra effort. The young man managed to bring down eleven, all of which fell, as luck would have it, right into the rhododendrons.

Swagger of course knew exactly what she had to do, and she disappeared into the undergrowth eleven times and came out with a bird each time. The young man said that there was one more, which the Earl was reasonably sure was not the case, but he asked Swagger to go in once more. No amount of persuasion would make her: she knew there was nothing more for her to do!

Swagger was mated to one of June Atkinson's dogs, from the famous Holway kennel which is renowned as a good working strain. Lord Northesk says that he made the mistake of using a dog of Ms Atkinson's called Lancer because he had seen Lancer working. "The mistake was, I think, that June is such a brilliant handler that she can make any dog look better than it really is."

Although Swagger had a lovely litter of seven, two of which Lord Northesk kept, none of them had the working ability of their mother. Later, he acquired Sparticus of Kentene from Joyce Munday. "Whilst he was still quite a pup," says the Earl, "my wife had him out amongst the sheep, with whom he was misbehaving. She shouted angrily at him, 'Come here you b..... twit and sit down'. He promptly did as he was told and so he was known as Twit ever since."

For Lord Northesk, Twit became a magical once in a lifetime dog, the sort one always dreams about. He could all but talk; he adored children, and was once seen carrying the youngest grandchild around the kitchen by his nappies. "He was tremendously brave, he had a magnificent nose, and he needed virtually no training at all."

Twit was a natural retriever and highly intelligent. He became quite well known on the Yorkshire Moors and, as a last resort when a bird could not be found, people would say 'Send for Twit'. "He was a perfect gentleman," says the Earl. "But he also had a sense of humour and on many occasions, when he was looking for and eventually found what was perhaps a disputed bird, he would take it neither to me nor to any other gun that might have shot it, but to one of the keepers or beaters." (It sounds to me that Twit was the perfect diplomat as well!)

Sadly, Twit died quite young and was replaced by Dykson's Rhum. Lord Northesk bought him from a keeper who had been used to Labradors. "He had been much too hard on him," said the Earl, "and had over-disciplined him to the extent that the poor dog was frightened of his own shadow." Lord Northesk felt very sorry for the dog and thought that, with care, he would eventually be all right, and the right sort of dog for his wife to use. At first nothing could be done with him so he was named Dum, but gradually he became more confident. "Although he will never have much initiative," says the Earl, "he is very good to work with and is very steady and reliable."

Roca Medlar came next, a dark coloured dog with a similar breeding line to the famous Twit. He was named Dee (Tweedle Dum and Tweedle Dee) – and the two dogs are the positive and negative of one-another. Whereas Dum is a reserved dog, Dee is tremendously outgoing. "Everyone must be Dee's friend," says the Earl, "whether they like it or not. Though not as brave as Twit, he has the same remarkable nose and tremendous stamina, and he is also good to work with. So when I have them out on the moors together, Dee works way out at a distance whilst Dum works close to. Between the three of us we don't miss much."

Lord Northesk says he would not be without his Goldies. "They are good companions and willing workers, and they are very good looking and wonderfully gentle. They are friendly creatures who have given me a tremendous amount of pleasure and can be taken anywhere. What else could one ask for?"

And I have it on good authority from an acquaintance of the Earl, that the reciprocal love and care he shows to his Golden friends is immense.

Fostering a Golden Retriever

There are many reasons why people cannot have a dog of their own: they might work all day; they may travel abroad frequently; they may not be able to afford the vet fees or hefty food bill – but it is possible to share the happiness of a friend's dog, as Ross McCarthy wrote to tell me. His canine friend, Bentley, has now moved away – and he has left a dent in more ways than one.

Dear Catherine

For six short months I had the pleasure of knowing a lovely Golden Retriever called Bentley. It all started when a young couple with two twin boys and Bentley moved near us. Bentley was five years old on the fourteenth of February. This wasn't his real birthday, but a sign of how much love he gave.

Before our neighbours acquired him he was ill treated. The hair all down his back had gone where boiling water had been poured on him as a puppy, yet he still remained so gentle and loving.

They didn't have too much time to walk Bentley so I took up the job before and after school. He had a very special friend called Suzie, a German Shepherd. They used to run for miles together, never getting tired. But in December our neighbours realised they couldn't stay in their large house any more so started to look for somewhere else to live. They announced they were going to move away. This caused weeks' of heartache and tears from both sides.

Eventually they moved, leaving us all distressed, although Bentley gave us something to remember him by. He pulled me into a fence whilst chasing Suzie; he pulled my gran over, breaking her glasses, and he jumped up on my mum hitting her against the wall.

I still miss Bentley, and hope very much that he will be able to move back here in the near future so that I can resume my walking duties.

Ross McCarthy (aged 14 years)

"The dog has an enviable mind; it remembers the nice things in life and quickly blots out the nasty"

Barabara Woodhouse

Show Champion Stirchley Saxon

It's so nice to know that the world is full of Golden Retriever 'nuts', people like me who are absolutely dotty about the breed, and who would travel around the world to meet the apple of their eyes.

Show Champion Stirchley Saxon is one such magnet, a macho man with enormous personality, and an international fan club. In 1993, at the grand old age of ten, Stirchley Saxon became Best of Breed at Crufts – and deservedly so, for he has good looks and personality in abundance. Like Samson, Saxon's great nephew, he has a wonderful line in chatter, and could charm the birds off the trees when he lies on the floor and tells you, verbally, to come and stroke him.

Graham and Brenda Hall, Saxon's proud owners, have had visitors from Belgium, Holland and France, and even from Australia. If they come to the UK, they make a point of coming to see him.

63

Saxon and Brenda his No.1. admirer - (Sh. Ch. Stirchley Saxon - Ch. Nortonwood Faunus ex Sansue Wanda of Stirchley)

"Every now and again," says Graham, "you get a predominant sire coming along. Saxon's grandfather was Camrose Cabus Christopher, and he was another one. These 'special' characters have something that is different to all others, they sparkle. They come alive when they're with people and doing the job they are meant to do. When Saxon is at a show he really enjoys the performance. He shows himself off and makes a spectacle of himself, barking and jumping about.

"When he was young he had a following of people who used to come to the ring just to watch him being a clown. They say in the show world that there's something undefined about certain animals. Desert Orchid the famous horse has it; Red Rum had it. I think it's charisma, and Saxon's brother Solomon has been blessed with the same gift."

The two brothers, Saxon and Solomon, live at home with Brenda and Graham, and three Golden ladies, plus a delight of up-and-coming young pups. "It would be difficult to imagine several males of many other breeds living together," says Graham. "But Goldens are very gentle with one-another and we never have any bullying or fighting. In fact, we often grit our teeth when they end up in the same class at a show, because they're always delighted to see one-other and make a great big fuss of each other in the ring."

Come and play

I also discovered the origin of another of our Samson's genetic predispositions when talking to Graham and Brenda Hall: "I was walking them this morning," said Graham, "and because it was raining I tried to turn round half way. Saxon wasn't having it. He made me complete the full walk by grabbing hold of the lead and pulling me in the right direction. We had a tug of war, and he won."

"Saxon is ten years old this year," Brenda adds. "And he's still a puppy. There are a lot of people who don't get on with Golden Retrievers – you tend to find Golden people are gentle, quiet people. They appreciate a dog that is sensitive, who can recognise moods and understand feelings. A Golden just couldn't survive with a harsh, aggressive owner. We are very grateful to have shared our lives with them."

And I am grateful to Graham and Brenda Hall. For they have, through thoughtful breeding, helped keep the beautiful nature within this gentle breed. I'm also looking forward to meeting Daniel once again. This adorable young man – a ten-month old puppy when I met him – stole my heart away. It must be in the genes!

Daniel is rather fond of potatoe peelings - (Stirchley Spartan - Blakesley Benjamin of Westley ex Westley Lizetta)

The Stirchley girls

Sebastian

Hey Good Looking...

Sebastian is a star: a television star. He's a handsome, huggable, gorgeous hunk of bristling muscle; he's a dashing, splashing, jumping mass of action and adventure. He's a glamorous Golden; a thoroughbred amongst thoroughbreds; a real male.

When Sinnhein Sebastian became Best of Breed at Crufts 1990, his film career really took off. Snapped up by Pedigree Petfoods, Sebastian became one of the world's foremost Golden stars, evoking more response to any advertisement than the doggie food company had ever produced.

I saw Sebastian on the television. I was mesmerised and totally star struck. I fell in love.

"Sebastian doesn't know what it is to be aggressive, or even growl on any occasion," his owner, John Clark, told me. "Sebastian just wants to be happy, and for you to be happy with him. Whenever anyone comes to the house there's always a rush to the front door to see who it is. The first thing Sebastian does is grab that person's arm and pull them into the house. Some strangers are a little alarmed because they don't know it's a sign of welcome!"

67

Sbastian - (Sh. Ch. Sinnheim Sebastian - Ch. Sansue Golden Ruler ex Sh. Ch. Sinnheim Minutemaid)

John Clark doesn't believe that Golden Retrievers are kennel dogs, which is why Sebastian, his brother Severiano, and six Golden girls live in the home with John and his wife. "They absolutely thrive in human company," says John.

John Clark believes that Sebastian inherited a large portion of his wonderful temperament and beautiful physique from his grandmother, Westley Mathia, a beautiful 14-year-old who is known affectionately as Moray. His mother, Show Champion Sinnhein Minutemaid is also a real character: "She's so much of a character," says John, "that we cannot watch anything on the television that has anything to do with horses, dogs, cats or any other kind of animal.

"There's a collie right at the end of 'Emmerdale Farm' and a Labrador in the swimming pool at the end of 'Neighbours'. She brings the house down. We have to put her in another room if we want to watch Crufts; she even barks at Sebastian and herself when their advertisement comes on. If you saw her you would know right away that she's Sebastian's mother."

John is justifiably proud of Sebastian. "Everyone likes to think they can produce an outstanding animal," he says. "I think we did it with Sebastian quite honestly. I'm very proud of him. I have an ancestor who was a gamekeeper on a large estate just outside Glasgow," John adds. "He was a great lover of dogs and he had a tombstone erected to one of his favourites when it died. The words on the tombstone read:

"He was, but words are wanting to say what. Think what a dog should be, and he was that.

"Now that's Sebastian as far as I'm concerned," John concludes.

Grigg

A Golden First

Grigg is the first Golden Retriever ever to have succeeded in the UK as a Hearing Dog for the Deaf. The Charity relies upon the donation of suitable dogs, and spare well-balanced Golden Retrievers are rarely offered. "We had two Golden Retriever crosses under training," says Claire Guest, the training manager, "but we had trouble getting them to wake up to respond to sounds!"

It requires a very special dog to become the ears of a deaf person. They have to be alert, steady, able to concentrate, and they have to be well socialised. "If a puppy hasn't been handled by various people or isn't used to lots of sounds and sensations, then they become more difficult to train," says Claire. "From a behavioural point of view they can be a bit shy and, as pups grow, they tend to become less friendly. If they are seven weeks old and nervous we may succeed, but if they are 14 weeks and nervous we have a real task to make up for what has been lost."

Grigg was donated to the Charity when he was ten months old by a family who discovered that other commitments were not compatible with owning a dog. "After assessing him," says Claire, "we found that Grigg needed more time to grow up. He went off to live with a husband and wife who acted as puppy walkers for us. They fell in love with him and were heartbroken when they had to let him go, so they got a dog of their own and resigned as puppy walkers. It takes a single-minded kind of person to be a puppy walker."

Claire and Jane, Grigg's trainer, took me to one of their training houses to watch Grigg in action. The house has been rigged with various types of telephones, door bells and alarm clocks so that Jane can simulate the sounds Grigg will hear when he goes to live with his recipient.

Training normally takes 16 weeks, but Grigg was kept a little longer while his trainers waited for his puppyish behaviour to wear off. Normally on the 17th week the deaf person will come to the centre for training, and on the 18th week trainers will go to the person's home and stay nearby.

For three days trainers work with that person in the home. After another three weeks they go back again for two days, and then they have a two-month break and go back again. The dog doesn't become an official Hearing Dog until it has been with the deaf person for three months: a dog is only fully trained when he has made adjustments to the environment.

Jane ran through Grigg's list of accomplishments, giving practical demonstrations as she went along. The first stage of the training was to get Grigg to respond to a small hand held 'squeaker'. As soon as he heard the sound, he dashed straight to Jane, and Jane gave him an edible reward.

Later it was emphasised that a whistle, and not the squeaker, was used as a recall device. "The squeaker is a way of training the dog to touch and it also helps if the dog loses confidence at any stage; you always go back to the squeaky to build up his confidence," Jane said.

"If you use the squeaky for recall and the recall becomes a problem, then you have lost your main means of sound training as well: two problems instead of one."

Jane took herself upstairs, set the alarm clock, and got into bed (a fine thing to do while I'm trying to talk with her – but all became clear before long). The alarm went off, and Grigg rushed up the stairs and put his front paws on Jane's chest. "If he were a smaller dog," said Jane, "we would have taught him to jump up on the bed." I think it's jolly nice of him to be so considerate.

The doorbell rang and Grigg went to the front door to check the sound. Fully satisfied, he came back to Jane, sat down in front of her, and put his paw gently on her leg. Then he led her to the door. It's the same process when the telephone rings, or when a cooking timer goes off (perhaps so that Grigg can remind the owner that the bath water should be turned off, it's time to go out, or that the meals on wheels person is due to arrive).

All the time, Grigg's training is being reinforced with reward: Jane's large pockets are brimming with edible morsels. "It would have to be a really naughty dog for us to admonish it," says Claire. "We might clear our throat loudly if the dog didn't get up to answer the phone, for example, but we never punish.

"If they start to think that this is a place of punishment they cease to enjoy the work. We always use positive, never negative. The dog has to believe that there is nothing on earth more pleasant than working."

By the time you read this book, Grigg will have settled down in his new home with a lady called Christine, her husband and child. Christine has been especially chosen by the Hearing Dogs Charity – she is able to exercise Grigg and give him lots of time and attention. At one time, the boisterous Grigg may have been looked upon as a bit of a nuisance; now he performs a very valuable role – a thing, sadly, that some humans can't claim to do.

69

Standerwicks are go!

Fifty-something Years of Golden Retrievers

There are three people in England who have earned the respect, and a place in the hearts and minds, of everyone who has had the privilege to share their lives with Golden Retrievers. Joan Gill, who has owned and bred Goldens for 58 years, and Daphne and Mervyn Philpott who have had Goldens for 30 years, have together produced 32 title holders, many personalities, naughty characters and intelligent workers. Miss Gill has a joint interest in Mrs Philpott's Standerwick prefix, and Mr and Mrs Philpott have a joint interest in Miss Gill's Westley prefix.

The name Westley is the hallmark of quality in a dog, and this strain has produced many beautiful champions in the show ring, as well as friendly and affectionate family pets to brighten up our lives. Miss Gill bred David of Westley, who was born in 1951, and who was the only International Dual Champion that has ever been. Joan Gill had her first Golden Retriever, Simon of Brookshill, in 1936. It is easy to understand, when you hear of Simon's incredible personality, why Miss Gill should have devoted her life to this breed.

"Simon was a great character," Joan told me. "He understood so much. He used to like to go to bed at 10 o'clock. On one occasion, a visiting friend said about six times that she must go but she continued to sit and chat. Eventually Simon had had enough. He went into the hall where her handbag and gloves were sitting on a chair, and brought them to her. She took the hint.

70

Sh. Ch. Westley Munro of Nortonwood, Ch. Westley Martha and Westley Mabella (1981)

69

"On another occasion, when a friend had been staying for the weekend and had packed her case ready to set off for home, Simon decided that he would carry the case down the stairs for her. He picked it up, took it to the top of the landing, and then it burst open and everything tumbled down the stairs. Our friend was not amused, and scolded him, so he went to bed and refused to say goodbye to her as he usually did. He had, however, forgiven her by the next weekend."

"We have had so many real characters over the years," Daphne Philpott told me. "Mathias of Westley was an absolute hoot. He had been a kennel dog for nearly a year when he came to live in the house with us and our eight-month old baby.

"I had the baby on the floor on that first evening and he tore into the room, totally unused to children. I really thought he was going to knock her for six, but he skidded to a halt and in fact, he never, ever, knocked her in his life. My daughter learned to walk by holding onto his ruff and walking along with him.

"Then we started to do obedience with Mathias. You could make him bark to order, so he was always asked to thank the judge at training class progress tests. He'd come out to the middle of the ring, put his head in the air, and go 'woof, woof, woof'. Everyone found this all very amusing but every time we opened a packet of biscuits; every time we opened a tin of sweets, then Matty was there voicing his pleasure.

"My husband asked him to speak quietly. He kept on and on, whispering to him: 'speak quietly Matty'. Eventually we had a dog with a silent bark. If you told him to do it quietly, he would bark with all the actions but making no sound."

Champion Westley Victoria – a very important dog in the history of Golden Retrievers – was, and still is, the top Golden brood bitch, producing eight English title holders, an Irish Champion, a Canadian Champion, an American Champion, and two others with two CCs (Challenge Certificates).

"Victoria was very placid, very easy going, but she always had a twinkle in her eyes," says Daphne. "If she didn't want to do something, she would sit and look at you and say, 'No. I'm not going to.' She was lovely to live with, and she adored children. She was also rather beautiful and had a wonderful head."

Victoria's mother was Champion Westley Jacquetta who was, in Daphne's words, a very good little bitch. She always wanted to please you; never wanted to do anything wrong, and she was always by Daphne's side.

"Poor old Jackie, she didn't want to go anywhere without me and we used to tease her about it. If I was standing in the garden and my husband offered to take her for a walk, she would tug away and come and sit by me. But if I was in the kitchen, then she'd absolutely tear after him to go for the walk."

Joan Gill told me about the comedy act involving the beautiful Champion Clarissa of Westley (who was the bitch that started this famous partnership), Jacquetta and Matty, in which each was asked in turn to say 'please' for their biscuit. Clarissa would put her paw on one knee, Jacquetta would sit up and beg, and Matty would do his silent bark: "They would repeat the performance as often as we had biscuits to give them."

Martha, who passed on recently at the grand age of 14, was another lovely Champion bitch. Martha liked, even at her advanced age, to sit on cardboard boxes, and when the sides gave way she growled at the box as it split apart.

Daphne Philpott has mostly Standerwicks in the house with her at the moment. "We breed two lines these days – Westley for show and Standerwicks for the field," she says. "I began by training Westley Jacquetta and running her in about four or five trials, and she won two Certificates of Merit. Then I got the bug for working, and Jacquetta produced a litter which included Champion Westley Victoria.

"Victoria was a very nice little bitch, good at picking up, but she didn't have the biddability of her mother. I was attending a lot of field trials at the time and very badly wanted a working-bred dog. Then Joan bought me Strathcarron Seil of Standerwick who I trialled a few times, and she got a Certificate of Merit and a fourth place, and I had my first ever Standerwick litter from her in 1979. This litter produced Champion Standerwick Thomasina who won eleven field trial awards and four CCs in the show ring, which was most unusual.

"Seil went on to produce more Standerwicks, including Ft. Ch. Standerwick Rumbustuous of Catcombe and Ft. Ch. Standerwick Roberta of Abnalls. When Roberta had her first litter, I had a puppy which someone couldn't get on with very well. She was fourteen months old when she came to live with me. She won a two-day stake and got a diploma in the Retriever championships before she was three years old. This is Evita."

Roy Burns, of the well known Abnalls kennel, later gave Daphne another puppy from Roberta, and the puppy became Ft. Ch. Abnalls Hilary of Standerwick who won her first field trial when she was two years old. The following year she won two two-day stakes in eight days and became a field trial champion at just three years old.

Ill health has meant that Daphne has been unable to trial recently, but she is hoping to return again with more promising progeny. Yet despite her illness, Mrs Philpott is out most days with the dogs. The puppies are trained for a short time every day, and the older workers are trained at least once a week.

"A lot of people work show-bred dogs and they work very nicely, but to go to the very top you have to have this really special breeding," says Daphne. "Our Standerwicks don't look as beautiful as the show dogs, but they've got lovely faces and they're very bright and great fun to live with."

Although Standerwicks are working dogs, Mrs Philpott has no hesitation in bringing them into the home. "I have the naughty Evita in the house with me at the moment, together with Larry, Maxi and Westley Lucinda, and she's an absolute character. She spends half of her life on my lap watching television, throwing her head back against me and dangling her legs over the side of the chair. Evita is full of fun, just like a Golden Retriever should be."

Field Trial Champion Abnalls Hilary of Standerwick, known affectionately as Larry, is practising standing on two legs in readiness for her next life as a human. "Larry stands on her hind legs to get a better view, especially if Daphne is disappearing somewhere," says Joan Gill. "She can stay in that position for quite a long time. I don't know how she can balance like that as she's a big bitch with long legs."

Joan and Daphne firmly believe that Golden Retrievers have kept them young. "We spend a lot of time playing with them and earning their confidence," says Joan. "Play is a great way to get Goldens to trust you and helps to form a bond. That's how you bring out their personalities. It keeps us young – and they just love it."

So gracious are these ladies that they are always ready to credit other breeders. Although, for example, Standerwick is one of the top working strains in the country, Daphne Philpott is keen to make it known that the Holway kennel is at the top of the tree in the UK. "June Atkinson has made up more field trial champions than anyone else," says Daphne. "Her record is absolutely amazing, and her dogs just adore her."

Now, it just so happens that someone has told me that the Westley and Standerwick Goldens love their breeders with a passion. It seems that love and perfection are inseparable partners.

A Special Friendship

Abby, now a very lively eleven year old, is a hopelessly addicted tennis ball chaser who gives her ball reluctantly to all but one. While most people must pry the ball from her mouth, Barbara Burg's handicapped daughter Beth needs merely to sit and wait. "Abby drops the ball next to Beth," she says, "and then she waits for Beth to feel it and then throw it.

"Beth doesn't see too well, so the slimy round things next to her are sometimes not perceived right away. If Beth should take too long, Abby pokes Beth with her nose to make her feel for the ball. Beth then gleefully throws it, anywhere from one foot to several, and awaits the return.

"These two never tire – they play much longer than the rest of the family for we get tired of the game. But Beth and Abby happily play for hours. It's a beautiful companionship. No-one taught Abby this approach – she just seemed to know Beth was a suitable game partner. We are happy for both of them."

Barbara, who lives in Malvern, USA, is a regular visitor to local schools where she, her pregnant bitches, and resultant young pups, help teach children the technicalities of the reproductive system.

71

Danny (Ch. Willyberry's Just Dandy) shares his lunch!

Barbara's most dramatic responses have come when entering classes with an autistic child. Initially, the child wants nothing to do with her, retreats from her, and she knows that she must not look at the child or talk or touch him. Aware that Barbara is someone new, the child takes no notice at all of the puppy.

"But," says Barbara, "by the time I leave the classes, the same child is talking to me, showing me pictures, and patting the puppy. Somehow totally comfortable with me now, it's quite a remarkable and wonderful change."

Barbara is a retired nurse who breeds maybe one or two litters a year, if at all, and considers the pups to be her paediatric practice. The family also includes a Blenheim Cavalier called Emily, three ducks, one donkey, two rabbits and five cats who all live in harmony with Barbara's Goldens.

"There are many fine kind dogs in the world – but Goldens must be way up on the chart of BEST!," Barbara contends.

Featherquest Sir Casper (Featherquest Phantom Pilot ex Nortonwood Carna)

The Mystery Golden

Rachel Page Elliott from Massachusetts, USA, founded the Featherquest Kennel in 1945. Featherquest Goldens are in the background of many present day breeding kennels in the United States, and though perhaps not all are identified by achievement titles, breeders know that the genetic bank contributed by Featherquest is a constructive ingredient to any pedigree.

Rachel, known by friends as 'Pagey', grew up with a wide assortment of dog breeds and first began showing a German Shepherd in 1939. Meanwhile, Pagey and her husband Mark had begun to hear about the Golden Retriever, a breed not well known at that time in the USA.

The Golden reputation for duck hunting persuaded the Elliotts to obtain a puppy from the Goldwood Kennels in White Bear Lake, Minnesota. This was Goldwood Toby (Ch. Toby of Willow Loch ex Goldwood Ditt), descended from strong Speedwell lines from which came many of the early Goldens in the Midwest and Canada.

Mark hunted with Toby along the Maine coast where at the age of one year, and with very little home training, the dog amazed the natives with his ability to retrieve every bird shot or crippled. "He was a companion without equal," says Pagey, "and an accurate obedience competitor and tracker, with nine points towards his bench championship, when illness took him at the age of seven. Toby was the first Golden to win the title of Utility Dog, which

During World War II Mark and Pagey moved to Indianapolis and acquired Banty's Pluto of Bushaway. "Chip," as she was called, was daughter to F. Ch. Banty of Woodend, the first female Golden to win this field title in America. From these two Goldens, Toby and Chip, the Featherquest Kennel was founded. Their second litter produced Pagey's first homebred champion: Featherquest Pay Dust.

Tennessee's Jack Daniels was another outstanding son from the Kennel's early days (Goldwood Toby UD ex Blonde Lady of Taramar). Danny was an eager, strong retriever who took Toby's place in the duck blind and became the first New England bred Retriever to qualify for limited all age stakes in field trials.

The Elliott's goal through the years of raising and training Goldens has been to keep a balanced outlook on the breed, not letting the pendulum swing too far either way from field or show. They favour a workmanlike structure with strong, not coarse, bone; a dog of medium size that won't tip over a boat or soak you in the duck blind because of too heavy or soft a coat and – above all – a reliable, tractable, temperament.

Of all the Goldens who have touched Pagey's life, she has chosen to tell us of a mysterious character who seemingly appeared from nowhere and then vanished. Perhaps this mystery dog sums up the life of a Golden for us . . . friendly, surprising, willing, accomplished, and able to make any act just that little bit special . . .

The dog was trotting towards the group along a roadside until they stopped to open the gate leading into the pasture where a few were gathering for field training with their dogs. Pagey didn't recognise this Golden, so she called him to check the identification on his collar. He was delighted with the greeting, and when she saw that he was owned locally she dismissed any concern that he might be lost. Pagey and friends went their way, and he appeared to go his.

"Our first training exercises were water retrieves using small boat bumpers thrown at various distances from the shore," said Pagey. "For the first dog on line, the short retrieves were no problem, but she balked on the more distant ones. After several vain attempts to encourage her, two unretrieved bumpers were left floating some distance from the shore.

"Since no boat was available, I started to call my own dog in the hope that he could remedy the situation. But just then the Golden we'd met in the street pushed through the brush, slipped into the water, retrieved one of the bumpers, and returned it directly to my astonished husband who was doing the throwing. The dog promptly retrieved the second bumper in the same way."

Pagey says that the Golden was not a particularly good swimmer, as he held the bumper high and splashed the water with his front paws, but he accomplished what he set out to do nonetheless. Then, without delay, he trotted around the pond, tail wagging happily, and disappeared out of the pasture.

"All of us had remained surprised and silent during the entire procedure," said Pagey, "but it was easy to guess what the dog was saying to himself: 'There – *I* showed 'em'!"

Her eyes sparkled with joy

Misty

73

Joseph Dainty, an American-based Golden Retriever lover and well-respected proponent of the breed, found it difficult to describe just one special Golden, having shared his home with many for the past 36 years.

"After carefully considering all my wonderful Goldens," he said, "I have decided to tell you about our second, Ch. Jo-Dee's Misty Day of High Farms. Misty was the personification of the fabulous Golden personality, exemplifying the traits that have made them so popular and desirable in America. Misty loved life and everyone with whom she came into contact.

"Her eyes sparkled with joy and she exhibited that beautiful Golden smile right up to the end which came in her 13th year. Our vet once remarked that she seemed impervious to pain – even as the end drew near she still maintained her zest for life despite the fact that she was suffering.

"I could relate a number of episodes to illustrate her personality, but one stands out in my memory. This was when she had her first litter. The whelping box containing her nine puppies was downstairs in our recreation room. If she heard a visitor coming, she would bound upstairs and beg the visitor with a proud look to visit her family. As her puppies were admired, Misty stood by with that famous smile on her face and her tail wagging merrily."

There are eleven Golden friends buried in Joseph's pet cemetery now. "I live alone since my wife passed away in 1989, but I still have one precious Golden friend to share my memories and happy times with."

Her Spirit Lives On

Golden Retrievers are action dogs, well suited to action people. Yes, they're quite happy to keep you company by the fire – *after* the walk – but they're even happier when out in the fields or amongst friends and onlookers showing off their refined ability in the obedience ring.

A successful dog in the obedience arena is one who wishes to please his or her master above all else. They understand that they must implicitly follow their owners' instructions such as stay when told, come when called, and walk to heel, and at more advanced levels they are able to distinguish between a variety of objects and retrieve the one with a designated scent.

Dianne Barnes of Bonner, USA, named her first Golden Retriever Brandywine's Free Spirit, and little did she know how appropriate the name was to be, as she truly was a free spirit who adored the applause of cheering spectators. Dianne wonders whether it's always the first Golden who makes the greatest impression, or was she just lucky?

"As Spirit grew into adulthood," said Dianne, "it became apparent that she was not the ideal Golden Retriever specimen. Her muzzle was too long and narrow, the topline terrible; her gait rapid and choppy – but her heart and soul – that was championship material! Spirit's joy in life and happy attitude was contagious and always brought a smile to the face of even the most disgruntled passer by."

The obedience ring was Spirit's stage. When she succeeded, it was with style, and Dianne was sure the judges overlooked minor errors in their scoring. Her best trick was the ability to prance in place. When Dianne was not moving fast enough to suit her she would increase her pace – vertically! The head and shoulders never left the correct heel position, but the feet would move up and down at a frantic speed, much like a jogger running in place.

"When she failed an exercise – which she did often enough to keep me humble," says Dianne, "it was usually to the delight of the audience. Such as the time I made a perfect toss of the dumbbell over the high jump and sent my dog. Spirit cleared the jump beautifully, picked up the dumbbell, looked at me, then looked outside the ring. She made a wonderful retrieve to a young lad standing outside the ring!"

Spirit had a penchant for rocks and though she would not chew or swallow them, she did retrieved them to Dianne as though they were the most wonderful of gifts. Not just any rock would do – it had to be under water and about 6lb in weight. As she walked in a creek bed or river edge you could see her feeling the submerged terrain with her forefeet. When the perfect specimen was found, her head and chest would disappear under water and up she would come with a small boulder in her jaws.

"When I moved to the property where we now live," Dianne remembers, "for some reason I began saving the rocks Spirit retrieved for me. In seven months, after Spirit had died of cancer, there were enough to make a large flower bed in her memory."

Great Dual Purpose Golden Retrievers

Apache

Spirit

Moe Saffell of Chester, USA, says that Golden Retrievers have been his whole life – and his life's work has been well rewarded. For Mr Saffell is one of the few people in the world to have achieved perfection in the form of champion class dual purpose Golden Retrievers.

Good looks are the domain of the show champion; intelligence and extreme obedience are the domain of the field champion. In the Rockcrest dogs the most coveted attributes are rolled into one. Almost all of Moe's dogs were of show stock from pet breeders, so perhaps it is Moe's training that has enabled him to achieve greatness.

Moe always started field training his puppies when they were five or six weeks old. By the seventh week they were swimming and retrieving on land and in water.

Moe lives on Chesapeake Bay, an ideal spot for dogs who love water. Moe's particular bay is shallow for about a hundred yards, so the dogs can walk around until it gets deeper and then they start to swim. "I will stand in the water while the dogs swim," says Moe. "One day I decided to sit down and cool my shoulders, and I got a very surprising reaction from Ch. Rockcrest Riparian Scout***.

"Scout must have thought I was drowning, because when he saw me submerged in the water he came over and grabbed my shirt and started to pull me to shore. I started laughing and trying to stand but I couldn't because Scout was pulling me and swimming so hard that I couldn't stand up. Once he saw that I was apparently in safe water, he let me go. I'm sure that we will never know what goes on in the minds of our unpredictable Goldens!"

Ch. Betaberks Rockcrest Apache*** was able to show off his remarkable abilities in front of the neighbours one day. "I was out cutting my lawn," said Moe, "and my neighbour called me to ask for help. Our properties are bordered by a large hedge and fence, and the neighbour's daughter had dropped a baby dove and they couldn't find it.

"The little girl was crying and very upset, and they wondered whether I might be able to help. Well, I thought that Apache could probably find the bird so I lifted him over the fence and dropped him onto the ground. He looked up at me and I told him to find the bird. I surely wondered what was on his mind. He was a qualified all age field trial Retriever so he must have asked himself where I had put the guns.

"But being a wonderful devoted dog he immediately started to hunt the hedge. After going about 50ft, he stopped and lunged into the hedge. When he pulled out I could see he was holding something in his big beautiful muzzle. It was the baby dove, and Apache tenderly gave it to me.

74

75

Golden Memories

"You can imagine what my neighbours thought. They were jumping with joy when I gave the little girl the dove – it was a little wet but very unhurt. The little girl hugged Apache until I began to wonder if she was going to let him go."

Apache and Scout were true stars whose fame will, I am sure, continue to shine until the end of time.

footnote:

*** The three stars after Apache and Scout's names denote that they are qualified all age field trial Retrievers – a rare and honourable achievement as there are so few show champions who are qualified field trial dogs.

Jassy was the first, and most adventurous, Golden Retriever Rosalind de Las Casas shared her life with. "Jassy used to tear about everywhere," Rosalind told me, "leaping from stone walls and high banks – even, to my horror, when about to produce ten pups!

"She was a great hunter of all the wild things that lived in our woods – rabbits, squirrels and foxes were always rounded up if they weren't careful. But Jassy's great fascination was for hedgehogs. She would arrive at the top of our lawn with one of these usually invisible creatures carefully rolled up in her mouth. Then she would carefully put it down and wait until it unrolled in a bid to escape. If it did, a pat on the nose soon caused it to retreat again."

Rosalind would rescue the poor thing and restore it to the wild. "But Jassy always found it again," she said, "however far I had taken it.

Jass needed a little extra training so Rosalind's husband took her to several classes. "He was most amused," Rosalind recalls, "because Jass would bounce into the row of assembled dogs and insist on greeting them all – even the snarling ones. She did learn one useful lesson: to carry and deliver a message. Whenever I needed to get in touch with my husband, who might be working far into the woods, I just wrote 'lunch is ready' on a piece of paper and Jass carried it to him with great enthusiasm.

"Chloe was quite different: very gentle and quiet and easy to train. She used to love to go shopping in the town. We were once stopped and asked for directions by a woman with a small child in a low push chair. The child had a choc ice, but most of it was over her face and hands. After I had directed the mother, there was a loud wail and we turned to find that the infant's face and hands were beautifully and thoroughly clean!

"Polly was perhaps the most beautiful and clever, maybe because we had a close bond together. Unable to drive now, I depended on her company more and she grew to understand all I said and did.

"Could one ever be satisfied with less than the beauty, cleverness and love of a Golden Retriever?," Rosalind asks.

A de Las Casas lady

76

An Honorary Golden

Jack – the consultant co-therapist

The more observant of you will notice that Jack isn't a Golden Retriever at all – he's a black Labrador. But, as far as I'm concerned, the phrase "Golden Retriever" means sunny, loving, caring personality. On this basis, we don't care very much what Jack looks like, do we?   (although he is remarkably handsome).

Jack, the Honorary Golden Retriever, has kindly consulted to help make a point: it's not the colour or the breed, it's the heart that counts. As well as a being small Labrador from gundog stock with a highly developed retrieving instinct, Jack is also a warm-hearted assistant to his owner, Dr Alex Yellowlees, who works at the Murray Royal Hospital in Perthshire, Scotland.

Jack became a co-therapist almost by accident. "He used to sit in my office or in my car," says Dr Yellowlees, "and patients began to notice him and speak to him. Very soon he became a familiar figure.

"One day a lady, who was the patient of another consultant psychiatrist, asked if I would mind if she took Jack for a walk in the grounds. After checking that she was suitable and reliable, and asking permission from her doctor, she began to take Jack out on a regular basis. The two seemed to bond remarkably quickly.

"Jack very soon became attached to her, and she to him. He's a very friendly, open, warm dog who likes human beings. The two rapidly became almost inseparable and he would carry her satchel when they went on their walks. Then the patient started taking Jack into the hospital shop where there is a little cafe, and they became very well known.

"This girl has been seeing Jack for three or four years now. She's no longer an in-patient, but comes to the hospital and takes Jack out as part of her programme of therapy. She had been very emotionally damaged and deprived, and had great difficulty trusting and relating normally to human beings. Her life was punctuated by overdoses and self injury – but her relationship with Jack has helped to change a very sad pattern.

"There is a considerable mutual trust and respect between the two, and an exchange of love and physical communication that was absent in the rest of her life. It is probable that Jack has provided one of the longest relationships she's ever had in her life. I would even say that he's helped to keep her going in a way that might not have happened otherwise."

Another patient, a woman with anorexia nervosa, a severe eating disorder, has formed a similar relationship with Jack, and Jack with her. "This is a mutual thing," says Dr Yellowlees. "You can see lots of trust, caring and sharing in their relationship. They have lots of fun together and he has allowed her to get close to another creature when she found this impossible with people – this patient was also severely sexually abused as a child.

"In this context, Jack is non-threatening. She can touch him and this is proving to be a major therapeutic tool in working with her. Poor self-image is a core problem with anorexic patients, so natural, free and spontaneous love from Jack is helping enormously."

Dr Yellowlees feels that Jack assists him in his relationships with most patients. "They can see me as a human being who has a friendly and loving dog. It helps them to think of me as less clinical; slightly more approachable."

77

Jack

Dr Yellowlees believes that Jack's gundog training has been a key feature in his ability to work as a co-therapist. "You couldn't just have a wild pet racing about the wards or jumping about out of control," he says. "Jack presents himself in the wards as manageable and obedient, and he obeys patients when they use the right commands.

"He is a marvellous dog and a perfect companion: gundogs are so accommodating. If I want to go for a walk, Jack says 'OK, we'll go for a walk'. If I want to lie by the fire, then he's happy to lie by the fire. And if I want to sleep in, then Jack says it's fine by him. He'll be a hard act to follow, but we plan to produce a son who will be as handsome and caring as Jack."

How to select your puppy

There are two basic types of Golden Retriever in the UK: the working dog, and the show dog. The working dog is leaner and rangier than the show dog. He probably *needs* to work, for he has a great deal of energy to be worked off. The show dog, on the other hand, is delightful to look at, but some say he hasn't got the brains to be a working dog (!).

In America, the aim seems to be to produce a dual breed – one that both looks good and performs well in the field. However, UK Goldens and American Goldens look different in many subtle and not so subtle ways. As an example, UK judges don't mind light colouring but would reject a Golden Retriever whose coat is very dark, or similar to an Irish Setter. In America, the judge would favour the dark coat and reject the dog whose coat was cream or nearly white.

Before you start looking for a litter from which to purchase your puppy, decide whether you want a working dog or a show dog. Then look at the prefixes in the puppy's pedigree to see which group it falls into. Those with Sh.Ch. and Ch. before the kennel name are predominantly show dogs, although the 'Ch.' has passed a basic field test. Those with Ft.Ch. are workers.

Reputable Breeder

Ensure that your puppy comes from a reputable breeder who cares about the soundness of the breed, the condition of the parents and their offspring, and wants to ensure that you will be giving the pup a good home. Indiscriminate breeding has, unfortunately, led to the occurrence of a small number of bad tempered Goldens – so take your time when choosing.

Virtually everyone I have spoken to has expressed concern about 'puppy farms' where mass production seems to be the order of the day. Here, Goldens and other popular dogs are bred for the money they will bring to the breeders. Little care is taken over the temperament of the bitch or sire, their physical attributes, or the compatibility of the match.

Bitches are often kept in appalling conditions where they are expected to produce litter after litter until they drop. Their puppies are shipped off to be sold at an early age – so you will never find the mother in evidence when you go to buy.

Please don't be tempted to 'save a puppy' if you suspect it has come from a puppy farm, for another puppy will take its place tomorrow. The only way to stop such cruelty is to stop paying the people who value life only in terms of the money it brings.

Take a look at Mum.

79

When you go to view a puppy, you **must** see the mother, first to ensure that the puppies haven't come from puppy farms, and second to see the type of dog you are likely to end up with. It is unlikely that you will see the mother if you purchase from a pet shop. The caring breeders I have spoken with say they would never let someone else sell their puppies for them: they want to keep in touch with every puppy they breed all through its life. If you want to acquire a show quality dog or a working dog, then it would be wise to attend a few shows so that you can familiarise yourself with the best of the breed. Alternatively, make contact with a respected breeder or your local Golden Retriever Club and ask for advice.

The good breeder

It is easy to spot a conscientious breeder when you visit, for he or she will want to make sure you are able to give the pup a good home. The good breeder will ask if the puppy will be left on his own for long periods of time; no doubt she will be watching to see how you react to the puppies: are you frightened by them, or too rough, or insensitive?

She might ask if you have children, and if so, she may give guidance on how to teach the children to behave in the presence of seven-week-old pups. She might even want to be sure that you are able to exercise the puppy, and adult dog, sufficiently.

You will be given good advice about diet, exercise and training. You might be handed a worming certificate and asked to sign a form pledging to let the breeder know if, for any reason, you want to dispose of the dog. You will be told about inoculations and safety precautions, and urged to telephone if you have any problems or questions.

Conscientious breeders will take care to socialise their puppies: there may well be a radio playing in the background or a television set. The breeder may also have taken all the puppies for rides in the car, so that your pup's first trip home won't be too traumatic.

All the top breeders I have spoken to tell me that *you* have to be pretty good to get one of their puppies! They go through agonies to make sure that the puppies they produce go into good homes. As Gillian Clark of the Canonbie kennels says, "All the people who have one of my dogs must send me a Christmas card and a photograph of the dog every year. Those puppies didn't ask to be born, so I have to be sure that I have chosen the right homes for them. Feedback also helps me to know that I am producing good, problem-free dogs."

80

Choosing your puppy

Only a person who is very familiar with the breed can tell whether any specific pup has show potential, and whilst the parents may be quadruple champions, this is no guarantee that their offspring will follow suit. Diet and the type of exercise a puppy receives will also have a great bearing on his healthy physical development. And the puppy that looks excellent at seven weeks may not be too hot as an adult.

81

The type of life you lead, and the home your puppy is to join, should play a major role in the temperament you choose. I firmly believe that the characteristics you see in your puppy on that first visit will show in the adult dog – if he is allowed to be himself as he grows.

Prudence barked at John on our first visit – and she is still a very noisy girl. Oliver was looking for fun – and he grew to be the funniest dog I ever met. Sophie was gentle and reticent. We didn't see her sense of humour at our first meeting, but she is certainly the quiet and gentle lady today with a laid-back sense of humour. And Samson was confident and rumbustious – and nothing's changed!

The rule, then, is to spend some time looking at the characteristics of the puppies you are visiting and matching those characteristics as far as possible to your own lifestyle.

82

Do you want a dog or a bitch?

It may be that the puppies are sleeping when you arrive. Give it time, and wait for them to wake up (a good breeder will understand your need to take your time – but don't overdo it, raising puppies is extremely time-consuming). Arrange with the breeder to visit a couple of times before the puppy is ready to come home with you. This will give you the opportunity to ensure that you have made the right choice.

Check that the puppies in the litter are clean and free of parasites. Are their coats thick and soft? Are they all alert and friendly, with bright eyes and a friendly expression? Or do they shy away from you?

Remember, puppies are new to life, so if you are allowed to pick them up, do so gently, making sure that the weight is evenly distributed. Give them time to get to know you, and don't make sudden or violent gestures – because you, as a visitor, are part of their socialisation.

Many people are concerned about the colour of the Golden they choose, for the breed ranges from cream to dark golden. Even puppies in the same litter vary in colour. Take a look at the ears, as it is generally thought that a puppy will eventually turn the colour of the ears.

I can find little to commend one sex over the other. Goldens, on the whole, are even tempered whatever the sex. Take a look at the health chapter if you wish to overcome the problems associated with seasons.

Preparing for your puppy

This section deals with what *you* must do before you bring puppy home, and what you might expect from your pup.

The first rule: put all your valuable items away in cupboards, or high up where little puppy can't reach them. You can't, after all, blame a Retriever if he does what comes naturally and retrieves your priceless pearls or irreplaceable trinket box. It may also cause problems for your pup if he chews anything that could cause him harm.

If possible, section off the garden so that puppy can roam around without getting near your prize hydrangeas or valuable shrubs. Our own garden is in an 'L' shape – it was primarily this that caused us to buy the house so that we could put gravel in one area, the garden in the other, and a gate in between.

The gravel is great when it's raining and muddy out, and the dogs are allowed in the 'posh' garden when the weather is fine or they are supervised. Incidentally, check that your small puppy can't escape through gates or fences which would normally hold an adult dog. Put a mesh over it until he is around four months old and too big to squeeze through.

If you are coincidentally moving house around the time you're thinking of bringing a Golden home, then Golden Retriever coloured carpets are a positive boon. This means that you don't have to sit looking at long golden hairs when you plan to have your feet up.

You may want a basket for your pup. An alternative to the basket in the early days, when puppy is chewing, is a cardboard box and lots of warm blankets.

Ask the breeder in advance about the puppy's diet and stock up. It is best not to change the diet the minute you get the pup home because this could lead to stomach upsets. Any changes should be effected gradually.

Toys are a ***must***. Initially, these should be soft toys – small towels, soft rubber balls, and so on. Make sure toys are not so small that they are easily swallowed. As he gets older, toys could include smoked bones, and larger indestructible toys (most Golden Retrievers will rip the more fragile pet toys to shreds).

A bowl for water, another for food; vitamin supplements (see diet section); and a brush, and you have all you need for your puppy's first few days in his new home.

Bringing your puppy home

You've probably travelled quite a distance to collect your Golden friend, and you will need to be prepared for him to be upset in the car.

Go in twos: one to drive and one to sit in the back seat with puppy on your lap. Take plenty of towels and kitchen roll to cater for the almost inevitable accident. You won't be able to stop en route to give the puppy a run (it's usually best to bring your puppy home when he is around seven weeks old, and inoculations are not complete until at least the twelfth week).

Your puppy will be tired and possibly dazed by the time you arrive home. Take him into the garden and allow him to sniff around. Give him time to adjust – don't allow children or other dogs to overwhelm him. Let them say hello quietly, and then wait for him to take it all in.

The implications of puppyhood

All puppies require a great deal of patience, and a large helping of tolerance. Be warned: that little golden fluffy bundle is a master of disguise. He looks as if butter wouldn't melt in his mouth, doesn't he? You just want to cuddle him and keep him safe, and he'll curl up in your arms and go to sleep, and your heart will melt.

But, now that you've got him home, the apple of your eye may well christen the carpet. Don't tell him off yet. He's new to this game.

Pretty soon he may discover a better game, reserved for those special moments when you are too tired, or too busy, to keep your beady eyes latched onto the sweet little thing. The game might involve eating his way through your expensive fitted carpet or Chinese rug. He might decide that your Chippendale table needs re-modelling. Or perhaps he's a landscape gardener in disguise, intent on re-designing the garden or digging up suspected buried bombs in the lawn.

If your puppy perpetrates any of the aforementioned crimes, then it's *your own* fault. Understand now, puppies do these things because they don't realise they're not supposed to. It is up to you to remove objects you don't want him to have; to give him your attention and your time until he understands the rules; and *never* to punish him. Smack yourself instead.

83

Samson Honey Monster

A new philosophy

You will understand, when you read the training section, that it is never necessary to act harshly with a dog. Dogs have been programmed to please.

My personal rule is always to be aware of the whereabouts of the puppy. I am watching all the time, and if I can't see him, then I am listening. (As I wrote this, Sammie was tearing up his Kennel Club certificate which had just come through the letterbox! He wasn't punished, we merely sent off for a replacement certificate. He soon grew into an obedient, non-destructive dog.)

In times of old, when men were bold . . . 'experts' suggested we break a dog so that the dog fitted in with our wishes. Things have changed now. We still want obedient, sociable animals. But we now realise that it is unnecessary to use brutality or unkindness to achieve the desired aim.

I personally can't see the point of keeping an animal if you are going to use its presence to make yourself into a horrible person. Kindness has never killed anyone. Some will say that animals, like children, need discipline — and they do, of course. There is a distinct difference between kindness and indulgence. Kindness means considering the needs of the animal and its place in society; indulgence generally means self indulgence, such as feeding the dog/child with an endless supply of cream cakes because it makes me feel better (forget that the cakes are ruining the little chap's teeth and making him fat).

Take toilet training as an example. The old-fashioned way is to smack a puppy when he has messed on the carpet. The new way is to ensure the puppy is taken out at regular intervals and warmly praised for doing his duty outside. Alternative methods involve keeping the puppy away from carpets, say, in the kitchen where any accidents can be easily cleaned, or in a crate using the dog's own natural inclination to keep his bed clean.

Although I appreciate that my solution might be slightly contentious to some readers, I believe in integrating the dog within the family from day one: happiness to me is a dog who is part of the family. You and he get the very most from the relationship in this way. This means being vigilant and anticipating what the puppy's needs might be in advance, accepting the odd accident on the carpet, and cleaning up thoroughly.

It seems to me that if you keep a dog locked in the kitchen or a crate, then you are only putting off the day when you have to teach him not to mess on the carpet.

Vigilance is a key word. Unless you know where he is, it's going to be quite difficult to teach him what he is, and is not, allowed to do. There's absolutely no point in telling him off when you find the contents of your handbag shredded all over the bedroom floor half an hour after the event. He won't be able to imagine why he's in trouble, because he can't remember that he did it. He will just think that you have a habit of appearing out of nowhere and shouting at him. You should have put the bag away in the first place, or known where he was and what he was doing.

Chappie was very tolerant with Samson

84

Be prepared: puppies have boundless energy

At ten weeks of age, Samson was a beautiful steady little chap who would sit when told, came when called, and very rarely had an accident in the house. He slept deeply, and played intently. But patience was still required in great measure.

Come 10.30 in the evening, when the rest of the household was exhausted and ready to go to bed, Samson would wake up, looking for the action. Chappie, Sophie and Pru would join in to help wear him out, roughing and tumbling with him, fighting (gently as far as the older dogs were concerned) over toys, and accompanying him into the garden so he could relieve himself. Eventually he would curl up exhausted, and we would stumble up the stairs.

Then first thing in the morning, Samson would trot up to the bed and ask in the most butter-wouldn't-melt-in-his-mouth way to come up with me. I would lift him up and then he would turn into a Honey Monster, biting and scratching any part of my anatomy that was unlucky or unwise enough to be outside the covers. My scalp usually came off worst.

My suppressed instinct was one of annoyance, and not inconsiderable pain. And yet, the first few weeks of a puppy's life are so important; they contribute quite considerably to his eventual character. Part of Samson's training was to learn to trust people, to respond to gentle but firm commands, to be fearless but obedient. Half asleep, I had to steal myself to react gently. Just as the three older dogs reacted with tolerance to Samson's sharp teeth, I diverted his attention to other mutually enjoyable games.

Here is another contentious issue: should you allow your dog on the bed? Well, I suppose it depends what you want a dog for. I have to admit that I love animals for themselves. They are not here to perform tricks, or to give me a sense of personal power, or to go with the decor. They are here because they intrigue me: they teach me about the workings of the mind in its most transparent vehicle. They make me laugh. They fill my life with sunshine (you can tell I appreciate them).

Some animal behaviourists say that you should never allow a dog on a bed because the bed is a tool you can use to establish your own dominance. Some folk say it is 'disgusting' to allow a dog on the bed. All I can say is that, having allowed our dogs on the bed, they now very rarely want to be there because John and I move in our sleep and get in their way. As fully-fledged members of the family my dogs are always kept scrupulously clean, and sheets are changed with amazing regularity. As for the dominance issue, there are other techniques you can use to ensure that the dog knows who is boss – see the chapter on training.

Every expert has their own idea of how to bring up a puppy. I take my lead from my Goldens who are as indignant as I am when Samson does something hugely antisocial. He gets heaps of praise when he does it right, and tolerance when he does it wrong. Neither I, nor the Goldens, smack, bite or rub his nose in it.

Goldens are very sensitive creatures, and I don't believe that it is ever necessary to hit them to get a message across. In fact, I suspect that physical violence is counter-productive with these gentle creatures. A cleared throat or raised voice has usually been enough to stop them in their tracks. Even then, you can't shout too loudly because Golden puppies can be very sensitive and may be extremely frightened.

85

Puppy's first night

If you have young children or elderly people in the home, you may not want to allow your dog to go up and down stairs. An enthusiastic adult Golden getting ready for a walk could knock a child flying. In this case, you will want your puppy to get used to sleeping downstairs, probably in the kitchen or other chosen area where he can do the least damage.

(In any event, it is not a good idea to allow your Golden to clamber up and down the stairs before he is at least six months old and his bones have strengthened.)

If your puppy is to sleep downstairs, then be prepared for a few sleepless nights. It is heartbreaking to listen to a puppy, all alone, on his first night away from the kennels and his brothers and sisters. He doesn't know why he's been shut up on his own. I have to admit here, that I have never managed to keep a puppy locked in the kitchen overnight.

By the time Samson came to stay, we had dismissed the idea of keeping a puppy in the kitchen. He came straight to bed with us. We placed newspaper at the bottom of the bed, and we lifted him down if we heard him in distress or, if quick enough, dashed into the garden with him. Samson soon settled in and we had very few sleepless nights, and no heartbreak. He was fully house-trained by the time he was around twelve weeks old, and his favourite place at night is now outside the bedroom on the landing.

For those who wish to persevere with the kitchen – and it is perfectly acceptable if you do – here is some advice from some people who have succeeded: Comfort can be provided by blankets, a non-destructible (stone) hot water bottle and perhaps a blanket kindly supplied by the breeder from the litter's bed (so he can still smell his brothers and sisters).

When the puppy cries, go in and comfort him and wait while, like a baby, he falls asleep. As soon as you tiptoe away, he will wake up and you must start again. Some people recommend soft and gentle words from outside the kitchen door – it never worked for me, but then I gave up after about an hour.

Some words of wisdom on this point have come from Joy Bawtree, who settled the puppy Benji down by taking off her dressing gown and allowing Benji to sleep with it in the kitchen. Joy says that on the first night, when he started to cry, she took her dressing gown off, and Benji snuggled into it and fell asleep. Again, on the second night, Joy took her dressing gown off when Benji cried and he went to sleep.

On the third night, she forgot to wear her dressing gown, so when Benji cried Joy gave him her night-dress and streaked upstairs!

It seems that Benji was perfectly happy if he could smell his new mum, and snuggle into her warm clothing. It's amazing how quickly a puppy learns to love you.

General dietary guidelines

Clean fresh water should always be available and changed once daily at the very least. Always clean the bowl when you change the water.

Essential nutrients

Proteins, found predominantly in meats, aid growth and energy. Carbohydrates, for energy, are found in cooked potatoes, rice, wholemeal bread, dog biscuits and mixer.

Vitamins and minerals, predominantly calcium and phosphorous, aid bone formation and development: it is important that your dog has the correct balance of vitamins and minerals. Problems can arise if you give too much, so it is rarely necessary to feed vitamin supplements to normal adult dogs.

Fat is another important energy source for dogs and, in the correct proportions, gives good skin, coat, and vitality. Too much fat in the diet will obviously lead to obesity. As an example, mincemeat is probably not a good regular source of meat as it has a very high fat content.

Prepared foods versus home cooking

Whilst some dog owners choose to prepare their pets' food at home using ingredients such as rice, liver, tripe, vegetables, vegetable oil and bonemeal, supplemented with cooked eggs, table scraps and wholemeal bread, there is evidence to suggest that home-prepared meals, although delicious, can lack balance. This is because it is very difficult to scientifically analyse the contents.

With some seven million dogs in the UK alone, it is in the best interests of pet food manufacturers to ensure that the foods they sell contain all the essential ingredients to promote canine health and vitality. For this reason, most vets will recommend you use prepared foods at the core of your Golden's diet.

The question follows whether you should use tinned dog food, or one of the complete dry dog food brands? It is likely that your dog will answer this question for you: some people say Golden Retrievers are stomachs on legs, but in our experience there are certain brands they will not eat!

Note, however, that not all dog foods are scientifically prepared. Look for the label on the can or bag which says 'complete balanced diet'.

A varied diet?

Some people say you should *never* feed your dog titbits: dogs don't need cakes and sweets, and you shouldn't encourage them to beg or even demand everything you are eating. Others say that we all like a treat now and then, and a dog is no exception. The question must be, when you offer or withhold that delectable morsel, are you serving your dog, or are you serving yourself?

It is said that a dog's stomach does not benefit from a varied diet; that it is better to stick to one type of food that agrees with the dog. But can you really harm a dog by giving him an occasional treat?

I admit that we do give our Goldens table scraps and the odd piece of chocolate, and they have never *appeared* to suffer as a result. The two major sources of stomach upset have been contaminated water in streams, lakes and puddles; and uncooked bones.

But whenever we meet a healthy elderly Golden, I ask the owner what they feed him. The answer, invariably, is that the dog is not given titbits, but he does have vegetables mixed in with his food.

I have to conclude, then, and after much thought, that foods which are rich in sugar, salt and additives are not a good idea. Erica Peachey rewards dogs during training with liver cooked in garlic – both healthy and delicious. Grigg, a hearing dog, was rewarded with small dog food pellets when I saw him being trained. So be strong, and reward your dog with food that is good for him.

Supplements

Tiny drops of cod liver oil and yeast tablets are highly recommended (yeast tablets are not harmful when given in excess and do not put on weight, so they are also a good training aid). Cheese, in moderation, is a good source of calcium. A few dogs develop diarrhoea if given milk and some are allergic to fish or fish products.

Some bones are very good for dogs, others can kill him. Large marrow, or knuckle, bones will give him hours of enjoyment and clean his teeth very effectively. However, they are best cooked to destroy any bacteria and avoid the likelihood of diarrhoea, and they should be taken away once they have been chewed down to a size which could cause a blockage if swallowed. Remove old rancid bones as the bacteria can kill.

Small bones, such as chicken or chop bones, should never be given to your dog as they can splinter, become lodged in the throat, or travel into the body and cause internal damage.

Specialist diets

Once you start to look into it, the whole subject of canine diet becomes fascinating. I have to add, that having looked into the subject very carefully, we have now changed our dogs' diet completely, so that it is based upon organically grown ingredients.

The famous holistic vet, Christopher Day, offered dietary guidelines when he treated Chappie for ruptured cruciate ligaments (see chapter five for Chappie's progression under acupuncture and homeopathic treatment). Like all wise men, Mr Day is neither dictatorial nor dogmatic when giving advice, but he does suggest that there are certain foods which help the body in its attempt to heal itself, and others which are not helpful.

Not recommended

Milk, wheat, colourings, flavourings, synthetic anti-oxidants, salt and sugar. Liver should not be given unless it is organic, and then only once a week. (It is interesting to note that a member of one of the police dog training divisions has since told me that many of their dogs develop diarrhoea when eating wheat, but they settle down when given wheat-free foods.) Mr Day also suggested that aluminium cooking utensils should not be used and plastic food bowls are not advised.

Recommended foods

Rice, rice cakes, porridge oats (either cooked or soaked and eaten raw), rye biscuits, potatoes boiled in their jackets, vegetable's (raw – grated or chopped, or lightly steamed), white meats such as boiled organic or wild rabbit (not red meats), fish (from unpolluted waters), raw green tripe (yeuk). All organically grown cereals, excluding wheat.

A vitamin supplement should be given to the dog eating an holistic organic-based diet. The Hay diet, where meat and starches are not mixed together but eaten separately, is also recommended.

Animal behaviourist, Dr Roger Mugford, has treated a number of dogs, including Golden Retrievers, who have suddenly, for no apparent reason, attacked their owners, small children or other animals. He believes that this problem is associated with liver dysfunction and can often be solved by a change in the dog's diet.

Dr Mugford contends that the protein content of the diet, possibly also the protein quality, is the main factor. He says that high levels of protein are often associated with tinned foods and home prepared diets containing a high meat content, and over processing of some tinned foods can lead to poor protein quality.

Dr Mugford has had some success treating certain types of aggression with a diet consisting of boiled chicken, mutton, fish or rabbit, mixed with boiled rice or mashed potato in a ratio of one part meat to four parts rice/potato. Importantly, a vitamin and mineral supplement is added (as directed by the manufacturer). For further information, Dr Mugford can be contacted through the Association of Pet Behaviour Counsellors (see listing at the back of the book).

Diet also plays a major role in treatments offered by the alternative vet John Carter. As readers of 'Dogs Today' will know, Mr Carter has achieved some astonishing successes where, in the words of the magazine's editor, Beverley Cuddy, "everyone else has given up." Beverley tells me that Mr Carter has even cured many dogs of cancer. For example, Sarah Jayne Whitlaw's Border Collie, Eve, was diagnosed as having incurable nasal cancer, but was treated and apparently cured with a special organic diet.

Beverley's own dog, Sally, is now in fine health, thanks to John Carter. Her heart was slightly enlarged and her liver was not functioning properly, but the vet said that nothing much could be done except to manage the condition. Convinced that Sally only had a short time left, Beverley called upon John Carter. An exotic diet of raw liver and organic vegetables, high-potency vitamins, nicotinic acid, powdered pig's pancreatic juices, organic carrot juice, and homeopathic thuja solution, as well as bottled mineral water, has helped the liver to rejuvenate itself. Beverley reports that if you could see Sally running in the park with her daughter Pops, you wouldn't believe she'd been all but written off a couple of months before.

Conventional Feeding of the Golden Puppy

At seven or eight weeks of age, when you first bring your puppy home, he will need a balanced diet of four meals a day.

It is not good to suddenly change your puppy's diet when you bring him home, as this will give rise to upset stomachs and add to the stress of the move away from his litter mates. Many breeders will supply you with a small quantity of his normal food to give you time to buy-in the correct supplies. If possible, check with the breeder and stock up before he arrives home – because you're going to be busy.

Each puppy varies in his appetite, so if he is still hungry, then give him more; if he leaves some, give him less the next time. If he refuses to eat more than one meal, I would be inclined to telephone the vet and ask for advice – it doesn't hurt to check with an expert. If the lack of appetite is accompanied by diarrhoea and/or vomiting, don't wait, consult the vet immediately. *Sickness in a puppy requires urgent attention.*

If you find that your puppy is not interested in the food at all, encourage him by sitting with him and offering him the first few bites from your (clean) hand. Don't forget, of course, to wash your hands afterwards.

Your puppy will probably take a few little bites and then wander off around the room, returning now and again to take in more food. This is because his attention span is very short at this age. You may find it necessary to bring the food to his attention once again. Remove any food he has not eaten within about 15 minutes, and make a fresh supply for his next meal.

88

Roy Bartlett decided he would stop the little terrors eating each others food!

Daily diet at seven to eight weeks

Your puppy's four meals should be given at regular intervals throughout the day (say, 8 am, 12 noon, 4 pm, and 8 pm). Don't give a puppy cow's milk as it will probably make him sick.

Meal 1:

One Weetabix mixed with half a pint of warm powdered milk and a teaspoon of honey, or Porridge sweetened with honey.

Meal 2:

Any of the following, as much as he will eat (generally in a ratio of 6oz of meat to 1oz of biscuit, gradually increasing as your puppy's appetite grows):

Tinned puppy food plus brown rice or wholemeal bread or puppy biscuits (softened with warm water).

Alternatively, use a complete puppy food which comes in pellet form and needs to be moistened with warm water.

Add calcium tablets in accordance with the manufacturer's recommendations. A small drop of cod liver oil will give him the necessary A and D vitamins. One or two yeast tablets aid vitality and help to give a good coat (again, follow manufacturers' instructions).

Alternate meals one and two so that he has four meals a day.

At *four months,* he should have three meals a day (only one of which is milk-based). At *six months* this should be reduced to two meals, and finally, at *nine months,* he will be able to cope with only one meal a day.

Some people prefer to stay with two meals a day for the dog's adult life, giving half the daily requirement in the morning, and half in the evening. If you are feeding your adult dog only once per day, give dog biscuits at other times as 24 hours is an unnecessarily long time to go between meals.

Natural feeding for the puppy

I cannot recommend that you devise a 'green' diet for your puppy yourself, unless you completely understand dietary requirements. However, I can recommend that you take a look at slippery elm gruel, a puppy weaning food from Green Ark Animal Nutrition of Galloway, Scotland. Green Ark makes wholefoods and herbal food supplements for animals, all of which are organically grown. The gruel contains slippery elm, maize flour, barley, marshmallow, dill and cinnamon. For further information, see Green Ark in the address section at the end of the book.

Quantities for the adult Golden

The quantity of food your Golden Retriever requires will depend upon his size: a large male will need more than a small female, for example, and a working dog will need more than one with a sedentary lifestyle. The manufacturers' instructions are a good starting point, but you should obviously reduce the content if he becomes fat. Generally speaking, biscuits and fat put weight on. Wheat bran and vegetables add bulk and stave off hunger pangs, but they are not fattening. Tinned obesity foods are available (from the vet in the UK).

Too thin needs to be avoided, too – you should be able to feel his ribs when you run your hand gently along his side, but the ribs shouldn't be free of meat altogether.

If you have more than one dog, either ensure that they are fed separately, or keep an eye on them to make sure Mr or Miss Piggy isn't doing the rounds.

Don't worry – be flexible

At six months, Samson started to decline his morning and mid-day meal, but ate his evening meal avariciously. He would then ask for food (by going to the food bin and barking) in the late evening. I could see no reason why we shouldn't adapt to suit him. We also found that Samson wasn't a bit interested in the Weetabix or complete puppy food. All he wanted to do was go and pinch the food from the big dogs' bowls. We overcame this by adding a small amount of the adult complete food to his bowl. Later we abandoned the puppy food altogether and mixed extra vitamins and malt and cod liver oil into the adult food.

We have recently changed our four to Green Ark Cereal mix. Sophie, in particular, has responded by showing more vitality and zest for life. She no longer wishes to touch other foods.

Keep an eye on any dog who seems to go off his food, but don't worry too much if it happens now and then. It may be he is feeling the summer heat, or he wants to give his digestive system a rest. Dogs in the wild often go for several days without food. Some people even introduce a regular fasting day – once a week or once a month – and they contend that this is beneficial.

Ultimately, you will know if your Golden's diet is satisfactory when you see clear shining eyes and a glossy coat, and he is brimming with vitality.

89

A mixer shower is a good way to bathe your dog

Grooming

Pretty Fluffy Goldens

First, ladies, take a look at *your* fingers. Sorry, but those luxurious long nails will have to go, as I realised the day I nearly poked my darling's eye out!

Second, ladies and gentlemen, hang those silk suits back in the wardrobe and get your sloppy joes on. You'll never enjoy your Golden to the full if you're worrying about creasing your clothes or attracting long Golden hairs. (John was once in a meeting and a chap said: "Aha! You've got a Golden Retriever!" John asked him how he knew... The Golden hair on his lapel, of course: the man was also owned by a Golden, so he knew from experience.)

We now buy our clothes to suit the Goldens: "That cardigan will never last, Sam will rip the sleeves with his teeth. What, you're thinking of wearing white? How long do you think it will take before it's covered in muddy paw marks? . . . You thought I was going to talk about grooming your Golden? Well I am now:

One of the very many nice things about Goldens Retrievers is that they don't take an enormous amount of grooming (if only I had hair like that!). Their coats are naturally smooth, soft and silky.

For the pet Golden, essential pieces of grooming equipment include a brush, a comb, some nail clippers, ear cleaning fluid (from the vet), a pair of scissors, and towels.

Brushing

Goldens only really *need* to be brushed once a week or so, but they enjoy it so much you can do it more often. (If you groom each day, according to some animal behaviourists, you are establishing dominance over your dog. Apparently, pack leaders have the privilege of grooming subordinates – now isn't that a nice kind way of telling them who is boss?) Regular brushing also helps to keep his coat glossy and tangle-free, and minimises the impact of Golden hairs on the carpet. Ours generally get a good brush in the evening, in front of the television (which we never manage to actually watch).

Use soft, gentle, strokes. Try not to bang the brush down on his body. A comb helps you to get down to the dense undercoat.

De-muddifying

Goldens attract mud like pins to a magnet, so you'll need to get the de-muddifying routine resolved as soon as possible – for the sake of your carpets and your clothes. Our four automatically sit when they come in from the garden and put their paw paws up for a towelling down because it has become a habit over time. Make it fun for the young puppy, and congratulate him on his good behaviour.

For more serious mud, we have installed a hot and cold mixer tap outside the house. This way, they can get as muddy as they like when out walking, and we simply spray their bottom halves when we arrive home, followed by a good, but gentle, rub with the towel. Sophie and Sam are particularly partial to rolling in horse manure and cow dung: the outside shower proves invaluable here.

The mixer tap doubles as a full shower in the summer, when the weather is kind enough for us to give them a complete shampoo and blow-dry. I would recommend an outside shower to everyone with a Golden Retriever (drawn from the hot and cold taps in the downstairs cloakroom, bathroom or kitchen), because it is incredibly difficult to lift a full grown model in and out of the bath. Furthermore, Goldens have a perverse sense of humour and they just love shaking any excess water over the wallpaper inside the house.

If you use the family bathroom, place a towel over your Golden before you lift him out of the bath. It would be a good idea to keep the bathroom door closed until you've dried him down so he can't run out and shake everywhere (which Chappie used to thinkwas an hilarious game).

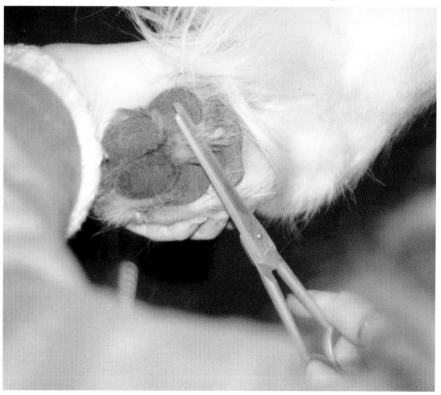

Keeping paws clean - remove excess hair

90

98

Goldens only really need a full bath once every six months or so, especially if they are able to go swimming in a nice clean river or lake. If you spot fleas or ticks, however, one cure is a complete bath using a dog shampoo containing a mild insecticide. These can be obtained from pet shops and vets. As with all chemicals, they should be used sparingly.

If you bath or shower your dog, use as little shampoo as you can get away with – just enough to work up a nice lather yet avoid unnecessary irritation. Avoid the eyes and try not to get water and soap into his ears. Rinse thoroughly. Stand clear while your darling has a good shake, and towel dry. If you have been forced to wash your little fluffy bundle in cold weather, finish off with the hair dryer (get your young puppy used to the hair dryer as soon as possible, but don't bath him until he is around six months old). Keep your Golden warm until completely dry.

Note: most Goldens will submit quite happily to the shower if you are only cleaning the bottom half. Once you start soaking his head, however, he will start to object. Lots of praise and encouragement is needed, as well as a little firm (but gentle) handling. Do the head last.

Nails

Goldens' nails need to be trimmed routinely, from puppyhood, to avoid problems with the bone structure of his paws and to make walking more comfortable. It is extremely important that you don't cut into the 'quick', a pink blood vessel within the nail. Take a look at your puppy's paws, and you will see that the nail grows beyond the quick. If you are unsure where the quick is, ask your vet or a 'doggie' friend to show you. Many people ask their vet to trim their dogs' nails.

Not only would it be extremely painful for him if you cut into the quick, but it will also make it very much more difficult for you to cut his nails in the future. If he's been hurt once, he's going to take a long time to accept your advances again.

Trimming

Unless you show your Golden, you don't need to do a great deal of trimming. Ours have their tails and undercarriages trimmed merely to prevent them getting tangled up in brambles, and around the ears and paws for their own comfort.

Use a sharp pair of scissors to trim the hair between the pads on his paws. This will minimise the amount of mud he carries into the house, avoid problems caused by lingering dampness, and give him a better 'hold' when walking across polished floors.

91

I don't like it!

For the show Golden, the primary concern is to show his body shape off to best advantage without leaving any obvious scissor marks. If, for example, he has a lion's mane of a chest making his neck look short and stumpy, then you may wish to use a stripping knife – very subtly. Alternately, use thinning scissors to trim underneath the coat, leaving the top hairs long.

The tail, if left untrimmed, can make a Golden appear out of proportion, with his tail very long in relation to his body. Use straight scissors to trim the tail; it's easier if the dog is lying down. Take the tail in your hand and locate the end bone, and trim half an inch beyond that (1.3cm). Cut down in a fan shape, leaving about four inches of feathers.

Stray or untidy hairs can be trimmed from the base of the tail, around the 'ankles', and around the ear flaps.

If you do plan to show your Golden, take him along to ring craft classes where you will be shown exactly how to trim him for showing.

Trimming in USA

Interestingly, the fashion in America is not to trim very much at all. The natural look is very popular, although minor trims are done to enhance the physique of the dog.

If you are planning to show your dog in the USA, take a look at the breed standard in chapter six. Examine your competitors before letting loose with the scissors.

Teeth

Hard dog biscuits and marrow bones will help to keep your dog's teeth clean. Also, if you get him used to having his teeth cleaned as a puppy, you can help him to keep them throughout his life. Don't use human toothpaste, because dogs dislike the taste. Use his own toothbrush, and scrape off accumulated tartar with a tooth scaler.

Students at Moulton College, Northamptonshire, give Sophie the full beauty treatment. **92**

It is important to get to know your own dog. By watching, you will soon begin to recognise what is normal, and when veterinary attention is required.

If in doubt, consult your vet. I am always amazed by my vet's ability to diagnose a problem when I can only tell her that there is 'something' wrong. Having said that, try to be as precise as possible when describing symptoms. I don't think it matters if the complaint seems trivial. In fact, I suspect that the vet would rather see you before a problem develops into something more serious.

Some conditions require urgent attention. Sickness and diarrhoea in a puppy, for example, should be referred to the vet immediately. Sickness and diarrhoea in adult dogs can also need immediate attention, depending upon the severity. If you are new to dog ownership and therefore unable to judge how serious the condition is, I would err on the side of caution and telephone the vet for advice. Where there is collapse, extreme loss of blood or seizures, consult the vet immediately.

Register with a practice as soon as you get your Golden and find out about surgery hours.

Accident

If an accident occurs and you don't know what to do for the best, leave your Golden where he is and keep him warm and comfortable. If you must move him (if he's in the middle of the road, for example), be careful of his spine and injured limbs. A blanket can be used as a stretcher: take great care as you roll him onto it, and use two or four people to lift the corners.

If he is bleeding only slightly, then it is best to leave well alone rather than increase the dog's stress by dabbing and fiddling. If there is a vast amount of blood, try and identify exactly where it is coming from and put pressure on the area. Even a cut artery will stop if you apply sufficient pressure in the right place. Do not try and apply a bandage, as this can cause more harm than good if not done properly, or if you tie too tightly.

Do not give him anything to drink (like brandy or milk). All vets should operate a 24-hour emergency service, but if you have difficulty contacting your own vet, or if you are out of the area, the police will contact the nearest available vet for you.

Anal glands

If your Golden appears to be troubled by his anal glands (situated on either side of the anus), you will notice him licking, and rubbing his bottom along the ground, and you may notice a rather nasty smell. Take him along to the vet, and he will empty the glands by squeezing. He may also teach you how to do this, although it can be quite difficult and problems will arise if you don't do it properly.

Frozen over

Pavement de-icers and car antifreeze are deadly for your dog. Clean your dog's paws so he won't lick them. Check under the car for spilled antifreeze: one teaspoonful can kill a Golden Retriever in around twenty-four hours.

Painting pain

If lead paint is sanded down, your dog can contract lead poisoning by breathing the dust. Paint, thinners and brush cleaners are poisonous.

Arthritis

Arthritis does not occur because the dog has spent too much time in water. A dog either has a tendency to arthritis, or he doesn't. The good news, then, is that you don't have to worry if your Golden loves a good swim.

The hips are probably the most common arthritic area, and this generally arises when there is poor structure and movement in the joint. If it is a 'flabby' joint and there is hip dysplasia, then there will be unwanted movement, damage to the cartilage and consequent arthritis. A minor strain to a wrist or elbow joint could also result in arthritis later on.

There is no known general cure for arthritis, although if it is located in the hips they can be replaced, and your vet can prescribe drugs to help alleviate the pain. (Alternative healers, some of whom are also qualified vets, *do* claim to effect near cures, if not total cures. See the end of this chapter for case stories.)

If the dog is already arthritic, the symptoms can be exacerbated if he is wet – so a towelling down after exercise will help ease discomfort. A comfortable warm bed will also be appreciated.

Breath

Bad breath is common in older dogs. Very rarely, it can be an indication of kidney dysfunction, but is more commonly caused by bad teeth and/or gums. I don't know where, but I read or heard that an overly rich diet with too much meat can be to blame. Don't take my word for it, but see what happens if you remove or substitute any particularly smelly dog food. You should really consult your vet if the breath is foul.

Burns

If someone drops a kettle full of hot water on your Golden, the quicker you cool the skin the better. Hot oil or warm jam are even worse than water because they will carry on cooking on the skin. If only a relatively small area is burned, put him under cold water – within milliseconds – and you will minimise the damage by a vast factor. If a large area is burned, you run the risk of putting the dog into shock if you deluge him with cold water: instead, place a cold, clean, wet towel on him – gently. Get him straight to the vet.

Flower bulbs

Gardening can be an extremely dangerous occupation for your Golden. Many plants are toxic to pets and some can be fatal if swallowed (hyacinth and tulip bulbs, for example).

If your dog is a natural born digger and you find him chewing on a plant or bulb, don't wait for symptoms to develop — take him and whatever is left of the ingested object to the vet. Plant identification is vital for proper treatment.

Cold turkey

Turkey and chicken bones break easily and splinter into sharp pieces which can cause blockages and perforate the intestinal tract. Symptoms of a lodged bone in a pet's system include loss of appetite, depression, vomiting and diarrhoea.

Cancer

If you see or feel a lump, get your Golden to the vet – but do remember that not all lumps are cancer! Some forms of cancer can be cured, but time is of the essence. If your vet can attend to the problem quickly he has a better chance of doing something about it. There are 'alternative healers' who report cancer cures. Indeed, I know of both humans and animals who have beaten the big C holistically.

Car sickness

Most Goldens seem to love the car but some don't. To overcome car sickness, take your puppy on lots of small trips to nice places so that he associates the car with fun and excitement. The shorter the trip, and the nicer the destination, the better. Medication, from your vet, can help during the learning process.

There are also homoeopathic remedies to help. A marvllous booklet, 'Homoeopathy for Pets' by George MacLeod (ISBN 0 907688 00 4) is available in many chemists and health shops in England.

Cystitis

This is very common in puppies around three or four months of age (normally bitches). If you think your previously housetrained Golden is being naughty, think again. The fact is that a Golden with cystitis feels a desperate urge to pass water; your vet can treat this.

94

Most Retrievers love the car.

Constipation

Constipation can be caused by many things, including lack of exercise, a lack of water, paralysis, lack of grooming, and a lodged bone, sock, or even a small ball in the rectum (it's amazing what a Golden will eat – ping pong and golf balls should not be regarded as safe toys for large dogs). It is not always easy to spot constipation in your dog, so you should generally keep an eye on his bowel movements. If he is constipated; if you see him straining, or if he seems listless or in pain, take him straight to the vet.

If the problem doesn't seem severe, give him a tablespoon of liquid paraffin and monitor the situation (some people suggest olive oil, but I am told that this is mostly digested and no longer oily by the time it gets to the place it needs to lubricate). Please don't confuse liquid paraffin with the paraffin you light stoves with!

Diarrhoea

Diarrhoea comes in many forms, from slightly loose stools to water. If you are particularly concerned about the severity of the diarrhoea, then consult the vet immediately. If the diarrhoea is accompanied by vomiting, then you should see the vet within a few hours.

Diarrhoea in a puppy is rather more serious and the vet should again be consulted immediately.

If you judge that the problem is not too severe, then you should starve your Golden for 24 hours. You may feel mean doing this, but it is the only way to get him better. Feed him small amounts of cooked rice and scrambled eggs or chicken the next day, and re-introduce his normal diet gradually.

(My sister, who is a veterinary assistant, says that it is not uncommon for people to feed chicken and rice *in addition* to the dog's normal diet. Alternatively, they have used processed chicken which is full of additives. The objective is to give your dog bland food which will allow the stomach to recuperate.)

If he is still ill after you have starved him for 24 hours, then contact your vet.

Ears

On the one hand, a well-cared-for dog should have clean, irritation-free ears. On the other, it is relatively easy to damage a dog's ears. So go carefully. Do not poke anything solid (like cotton buds) into them, or delve too deeply. Proprietary drops can be used, but only if really necessary. It is well worth taking your vet's advice on how/when to clean your Golden's ears.

Symptoms of ear trouble include constant scratching around the ears, head shaking, and ears being rubbed along the ground. If your Golden does any of these, see if you can find the cause of the trouble. Place him under a strong light and have a look – it might be a thorn or a piece of grass that can be easily removed.

If the problem has come on suddenly and seems acute, contact your vet; delays can cause problems. Do not use drops in these circumstances.

Haematoma

This is a blood blister – in this instance found in the ear flap. It is commonly caused when the dog shakes his head and the ear flaps jerk violently, or by scratching, a bite, or a blow. The ear flap will swell up like a balloon. Until recently, an operation was required to cure the problem. Both of Chappie's ears required surgery due to haematoma and, although he doesn't have obvious cauliflower ears, they are now slightly inflexible and knotty. The good news is that a new method of treatment, avoiding surgery, has been used with some success.

Poisonous plants

autumn crocus leaves - daffodil bulbs - English ivy leaves and berries - foxglove leaves - larkspur leaves and seeds - lily of the valley leaves and flowers - oleander (all parts) - rhododendron leaves.

Poisonous substances

amphetamines (diet pills) - arsenic (herbicides) - barbiturates (sleeping pills, sedatives) - metaldehyde (snail bait) - strychnine and thallium (rat poisons) - theobromine (chocolate) - organophosphates (flea, ant, roach and tick sprays)

Eating

Try not to exercise your Golden immediately after a meal: his stomach could 'flop over' – or twist – with a condition called gastric torsion, and this can kill him. Having said that, I know it's difficult to stop your Golden playing after a meal, but you should certainly not take him on a massive hike on a full stomach.

Symptoms: a great increase in intra-abdominal pressure so that the belly is as tight as a drum (ballooning), and the dog will try to vomit but won't be able to. If you can catch it, even in quite advanced stages, the vet can operate and turn the stomach round. Get him straight to the vet – within minutes.

It should be noted, lest you are alarmed, that this complaint is fairly uncommon with Goldens but more common in some other breeds.

Bird baths and feeders

Bird droppings can cause seizures, coma or death if eaten by your dog, and especially if they are consumed in a water base such as a birdbath or water dish. Don't allow your Golden to snoop around bird feeders, munch on bird seed, or otherwise risk contact with infected birds or their faeces.

Exercise

I thought that you shouldn't walk your Golden puppy very far at all, and that half a mile is the maximum. I've also read that you should always walk the puppy on a lead. The reason? Because, I've been led to believe, their bones are too soft for anything more arduous.

I asked my vet, and she said: "As long as inoculations are complete and you stop before the puppy gets tired (not after), he should be fine. A three mile walk should do him more good than harm. A fairly long walk on the lead is better than a short sharp walk off the lead, because this builds up stamina."

And yet . . . what a complex world we live in . . . it is thought that too much exercise before a puppy is nine to 12 months old can be associated with hip dysplasia. The key is not to drag him along with you, but plan your route in advance so that you know the puppy will not be tired-out before you get home.

Eyes

You can tell a lot from your Golden's eyes. If they seem sore, or there is a discharge, it may be symptomatic of a general illness. For this reason, don't simply try bathing – get him along to the expert.

If one eye is sore or closed, take a look and see if there is a grass seed or other physical irritant in the eye. It can be removed with a piece of tissue or tweezers if your dog can be held steady. If he won't co-operate, get him to the vet as soon as possible to avoid any damage to the eye.

If there is a liquid irritant in the eye such as washing up liquid or bleach, rinse with as much clean warm (not hot) water as possible to dilute it, and then take him to the vet.

Cataract

Certain cataracts are hereditary in Golden Retrievers and affect the dog's sight. Breeders have for many years been working to remove the fault from the breed. If you wish to breed from your Golden, you must have his or her eyes examined by an expert. In England, the expert is appointed by the British Veterinary Association. As with hip dysplasia, a clear parent will not always produce clear offspring, and vice versa.

Some cataracts are so minor that they don't affect the sight. You might be forgiven, then, for assuming that if your dog can see all right, it's acceptable to breed from him or her. Wrong. *No* Golden should be bred from without a current eye certificate.

Cataracts can be operated upon, although many dogs with hereditary cataracts also have hereditary retinal defects. Your vet will advise whether your Golden should be referred for surgery.

False pregnancy

Many bitches, two or three months after a season (when they would normally have had puppies), suffer a hormonal imbalance which makes the bitch believe she is going to have puppies, or that she already has puppies.

Some bitches respond by producing milk. Others, whilst they don't produce milk, do suffer from the psychological effects. She may shuffle up papers and try to make nests, dig holes in the garden or sofa and bury herself, ruin carpets, and hoard toys (especially squeaky toys) and shoes. She may even regurgitate food as if to feed her pups.

The false pregnancy causes great upset to the bitch but it can be easily cured with hormonal treatment prescribed by your vet. Don't be deceived into thinking you can cure her by allowing her to have a litter. She will merely have one real pregnancy, and the next time it will be just as bad.

Feet

If your Golden starts limping, take a look at the foot. It may be that he's stepped on a thorn which can be easily removed. Run your fingers along the pads, and between the toes to see if you can find anything, and take a look at his claws which might be split or in need of trimming.

If there's profuse bleeding, bandage it and get him along to the vet as quickly as possible. A child's sock, some cotton wool, and packaging tape make a good temporary bandage. Do not tie too tightly, but make sure it is tight enough to stay on until you reach the vet.

Fleas

If your Golden is scratching a lot, then it's possible he has picked up some fleas. Brush his coat backwards and see if you can spot any. If you don't see any adult fleas, you might see flea droppings which are typically about 1mm long and comma shaped.

The best cure is a bath using a dog shampoo with a mild insecticide. It is imperative that you treat other cats and dogs in the house at the same time, wash bedding, and de-flea the house too – your vet can supply the appropriate arsenal for attack.

If you have followed all of the above advice, but your Golden is still scratching, consult your vet. Itching can also be caused by mites, lice, or an allergy, so you need expert advice.

Out alone

Dogs who are allowed to run loose can be run over, poisoned, trapped, injured by animals or people, stolen or sold for experimentation. They can also worry farm animals and children, or cause road accidents. Don't let your dog out alone. Make sure he can be identified if he gets lost. A farmer is, under English law, entitled to shoot your dog if he *thinks* it is worrying his stock.

The British Dangerous Dogs Act entitles law enforcers to imprison and kill a dog and prosecute its owners if the animal is deemed to be out of control or dangerous.

Heartworm

Hips

Canine heartworm disease is mentioned here as it can be the source of much heartbreak in warmer climates. It is a potentially fatal condition for dogs who live in countries where mosquitoes are present (it is not a problem, I am glad to say, in mild climates such as the UK). Where heartworm is known to occur, dogs must be tested for the disease, and those with a negative test should then receive preventive medication.

In addition to damaging the dog's heart, the worms also attack the lungs and other organs, causing death if the disease is untreated. Signs of canine heartworm include strained breathing, reduced exercise tolerance and coughing. In advanced cases, the dog may cough up blood, develop an enlarged abdomen and have difficulty breathing at rest.

Treatment of unprevented heartworm disease requires injections to kill the adult worms. This can be very tough on the rest of the dog, so prevention is a far better, and easier, course of action. Preventative action also eliminates the dog as a potential source.

Small isn't always beautiful

Golf balls, old socks, shoes, discarded slippers, sticks, plastic flower pots, ribbons, ropes . . . irresistible toys? They could just kill your friend if swallowed whole, or in pieces.

Hip dysplasia has been found to occur in Golden Retrievers, and conscientious breeders are working to make the condition far less common. Generally, hip dysplasia means that the hip joint develops incorrectly. It can cause pain in a puppy as young as nine months old (in which case an operation can often help), and arthritis in older age.

Certainly if you are planning to breed from your Golden, you should have his or her hips 'scored'. To do this, the Golden must be over a year old, and taken to the vets and x-rayed under general anaesthetic. There is always a risk to your dog – albeit small – when under anaesthetic. Pat Bartlett, whose beautiful bitch, Bo, failed to come out from the anaesthetic after having her hips scored, has asked me to point out that a small number of vets are able to x-ray the hips without anaesthetic, but they must have invested in special equipment to do so.

From the practising vet's point of view, x-rays without anaesthetic are extremely difficult and time-consuming, and are prone to cause professional embarrassment because the sedated dog often moves just at the wrong time. This means another trip to the vet and a repetition of the exercise.

The x-rays are sent by the vet to an official panel of scrutineers (to maintain consistency of judgment). Each hip is given a rating of between 0-53. A zero rating represents top marks (0:0 would be perfect). The average for Golden Retrievers in the UK at the time of writing is 19.33, from a total of 11,337 dogs (British Veterinary Association/Kennel Club scheme).

The BVA/KC recommends that all breeders wishing to control hip dysplasia should breed only from animals with scores well below the breed mean. The sires employed should be ones whose progeny have had consistently low scores, whenever such dogs are available. Owners who wish to breed from a pet bitch should follow the same advice, since to use animals with higher scores represents a greater risk.

Sadly, Pru's hip score came to 14:24 (14 in the right hip and 24 in the left: a total of 38 out of 106). This put Pru well above the breed average and we decided not to breed from her. Despite this, Pru's health is excellent, and at six years of age she can run and jump with no problems. We're keeping our paws crossed for the future.

It is worth noting that both Pru's parents had excellent hip scores in their own right, and I have been told that the parents' hip rating seems to be no predictor of their puppies' hips.

Some people continue to breed from dogs and bitches with poor hip scores where other qualities are extremely good. Beware, though: you need to know what you are doing if you make this decision. Our vet says that you are playing Russian roulette, for whilst the initial litter might come out ok, successive generations are usually even worse. The result: you are enforcing the problem within the breed.

Neutering

Poison

Spaying

Spaying can help reduce the risk of pyometra and the incidence of mammary tumours. If the bitch is spayed before the onset of the second season, the instances of mammary tumours are massively reduced. Whilst mammary tumours are not always malignant, they're a bit like mushrooms and keep on spreading. Eventually they can burst and ulcerate and there is a limit to how many operations the vet can perform.

The disadvantages of spaying are that the bitch will have a lower metabolic rate and – if fed the same amount – will be more likely to put on weight. If the bitch subsequently develops arthritis, the extra weight will add to the problems. She may also develop a woolly coat and poor skin, which is why show bitches are not spayed. In later life she may develop a urinary incontinence due to a shortage of the correct hormones. Hormone replacement therapy can help, but it isn't a hundred per cent.

The conclusion is . . . there are pros and cons for each course of action. Vet Ann Hayes admits that she is unable to decide whether to spay her own bitch.

Family planning

Bitches can now be prevented from coming into season very successfully with the aid of a regular family planning injection. Importantly, if you decide to breed from your bitch at a later stage, the injections can be stopped. If you wish to consider this remedy, consult your vet immediately after the first season.

To be worthy of your Golden Retriever, you must take measures which prevent accidental pregnancy.

Castration

Have you noticed how male humans react badly to the thought of castrating their dogs? They seem to take it so personally!

There are two positive gains to be had from castration. The first is that it will stop him running after bitches (if he's that way inclined), and as a supplementary consideration, it may improve his temperament if he's an aggressive dominant dog. If, however, he's got into the habit of being a grumpy unpleasant dog, the operation may not change a thing.

Secondly, castration reduces prostate troubles and the incidence of anal adenomas (growths around the anus) which can be most unpleasant for older dogs.

The disadvantages are similar to those experienced by spayed bitches: woolly coat, poor skin, lower metabolic rate (reduce the quantity of food).

Keep pets away from any domestic or garden chemicals. If you live in a town or a city where there is a great deal of litter (particularly near food outlets) it may be an idea to muzzle your dog. Litter attracts rats and humans may put poison down to kill them. A soft muzzle will stop your Golden licking that poison. Antifreeze also poisons dogs.

It is very difficult to treat a poisoned animal unless you know exactly what has poisoned him. If your Golden starts vomiting or collapses he needs to be taken to the vet immediately.

If you see him swallowing a poison, pour a grape-sized washing soda crystal down his throat, or milk if the substance is corrosive. The crystals are much more effective than salt water, but do not give him anything at all if he is unconscious. Contact the vet immediately, and take the poison or its packaging with you.

95

Sophie's coat went "woolly" after she was spayed

Prostate gland

The prostate is a small gland near the male bladder which can enlarge in older dogs and cause considerable pain. A major symptom is that the dog will start to strain when he passes motions. Very rarely you will see blood coming from the penis, or in his urine. The control can be to administer female hormones; vets usually prefer to castrate. The operation is, my vet tells me, less traumatic than having a painful prostate.

Pyometra

Pyometra is a degenerate uterus or womb which can become infected. An operation to remove the womb is invariably needed. Symptoms may include discharge or a marked increase of water consumption. It is an extremely serious condition which, if left untreated, will cause death. Many vets recommend that you spay your bitch when she is young to prevent the onset of the infection in middle age (see 'neutering').

Rabies

We in the UK are thankful that rabies is not an issue, although cases are occasionally reported in human beings returning from abroad. Many fear that it will be impossible to keep rabies out now the Channel Tunnel physically connects us to Europe, and there are (unsubstantiated) rumours that quarantine requirements will change. Already, legislation is beginning to soften, and now certain classes of dogs and cats may enter Britain without quarantine.

The only reliable way to confirm that an animal has rabies is to destroy it and obtain brain cells for testing. The rabies incubation period varies, so a live infected animal can develop the disease and its symptoms any time within a six month period. Hence the current stringent quarantine laws.

Rabies is caused by a virus which produces fatal inflammation of the brain. The virus is carried in the saliva of an infected animal and is passed to a healthy animal or human being through a bite from the carrier, or through any open wound or mucous membrane which is exposed to the infected saliva.

Symptoms vary between groups of animals, but generally, infected animals are likely to refuse food, exhibit a general nervousness and may be sensitive to bright light and sudden noise. In the second stage they may bite savagely at anything that moves near them. (Interestingly, rabid cats are more likely than dogs to bite people: not all rabid animals are aggressive.) In the third stage, the animal becomes uncoordinated, paralytic and may appear to be in a stupor. The animal's throat muscles are paralysed, resulting in greater quantities of infected saliva in and around the mouth.

96

Sticks

Ticks

The animal is likely to expose more people to the disease during the third stage as many people, unaware of what is wrong with them, have handled the animals in an attempt to help.

At the time of writing, the Centres for Disease Control in the USA report that there hasn't been a single case of human rabies attributable to a rabid dog or cat since 1979. Vaccines have also been 100% effective in preventing rabies in exposed humans.

Vaccination for your dog is vital where rabies is known to be a threat. Pets should not be left outside unattended and, if you think your Golden has been in contact with a rabid animal, wear rubber gloves if you wish to examine him to avoid contact with saliva.

Try to discourage your Golden from playing with sticks; take a safe toy out with you on walks instead. The worst scenario is that it could stick in the ground when you throw it. He can run onto it, and it could seriously damage his throat. A Frisbee or a large ball is unlikely to do this, whereas a stick could kill him.

Ann Hayes advises that it is not quite so bad if your Golden finds his own nice smooth stick – they do love to carry them! Try to resist throwing it for him, though.

Lyme disease, so called because it is thought to originate in Lyme, USA, can cause major problems in the States, but it is also known to occur elsewhere, including the UK. The perpetrators are certain species of ticks (sheep tick in the UK, deer tick in the USA), who bite both humans and animals, and sometimes – but not always – pass on the disease.

If left untreated in the human, Lyme disease can lead to problems with the nervous system, heart problems and arthritis. Animals, including dogs, cows and horses, can develop a fever; swollen, hot and painful joints; intermittent lameness and poor appetite. There is no evidence that the disease can be spread directly from animals to humans.

The ticks tend to be active in wooded, grassy and marshy areas during the summer season. Certainly, where the disease is prevalent, long-sleeved shirts and long trousers tucked into socks should be worn.

An infected tick must be attached for between 18 and 24 hours before it can transmit the bacteria. The advice is to buy tick treatment from the vet. Never pull them out as they inject their body contents as you squeeze them, but get your dog to the vet, or yourself to the doctor. Some ticks are very small and difficult to spot, so if either of you have been in a high risk area and feel or look poorly, seek immediate medical attention.

Fertilisers

Many lawn and garden fertilisers and pesticides are poisonous and can cause liver and kidney disease in your dog. Keep him off treated areas until chemicals have soaked in completely, as they can be absorbed through skin or licked off paws and fur.

Vaccination

Vaccinations are given annually. In the UK they protect your Golden from the nasty canine diseases of distemper, parvovirus, leptospirosis and hepatitis. The same applies to other countries, plus heartworm and rabies where they are present.

Puppies who are in contact with dogs outside the family can be vaccinated from two weeks of age, although this is exceptional. Sometimes the breeder will have puppies vaccinated at six weeks, or the new owner will start the first course when the pup is ten weeks old, ending when he is twelve weeks old. Other vets use vaccines that require a first injection at ten weeks, another at fourteen weeks and a third at twenty weeks. This is purely a matter of the brand of vaccine used – both are equally effective.

Your vet will ask you to keep the puppy indoors or in your garden for a period after the last injection. This can be for about a week, but depends upon the particular vaccine used.

Thereafter, the vaccination is repeated every year. Some dogs, which are considered to be high risk, are vaccinated every six months.

Vaccination is not mandatory, although Kennels sometimes refuse to accept dogs who have not been vaccinated. I do know of people who prefer not to vaccinate their pets.

Kennel cough can occur where dogs meet together in groups. Consult your vet several weeks before you plan to put your dog in kennels or to attend a show. Some kennels now insist upon a kennel cough vaccination before the dog will be admitted. Kennel cough is a name given to a wide range of infective agents, mainly bacteria and viruses, so even if vaccinated your Golden may get a very mild version.

Water

If your dog suddenly begins to drink a lot more water (say, three bowls a day instead of one), it is possible that he has a problem with his kidneys or diabetes, or pyometra in a female. Again, get him along to the vet as soon as possible for a check-up, taking a fresh urine sample with you (the dog's, not yours!). In the meantime, do not try to limit water consumption – he's obviously drinking it for a reason.

Not what the vet ordered

Paracetamol is toxic to dogs. Aspirin helps contain pain, but do not give it to your dog if he is taking other medication. Check with your vet.

Weight

Obesity in a dog causes a strain on the legs and on the heart, amongst other things. It's uncomfortable, and the dog isn't terribly happy. If he's grossly overweight the skin will hang in flaps, rub, and may cause eczema and soreness.

An English adult Golden Retriever male should weigh between 70- 80lbs (5lbs less in the USA). A bitch should weigh between 60- 70lbs (up to 65lbs in the USA). To check your dog's weight at home, stand on the scales and weigh yourself, then pick the dog up and weigh both of you. The dog's weight is the difference between the two.

Too hot to handle

Heat stroke can be caused by exercise or by the temperature inside a car on a summers day. It can be fatal. If your dog is overheated, apply cool water all over his body and apply ice packs to only his head, neck and chest. Let him lick ice cubes or ice cream and get him to a vet immediately. Do not leave your dog in a car in hot weather —   this is equivalent to cooking him in an oven.

Worming

Oh dear, this business of dog business is causing such a massive fuss these days. People are driven to frenzied hysteria, either in defence of their pets, or in outrage against the waste products of other people's pets. Thanks to media flame-fanning, the general public now believes that all dogs, and all dog messes, cause dreadful diseases. This is not true: it is a distortion of the facts.

And yet, and yet . . . is it really fair to expect children, or adults, to dodge dog poo in the park, or slip in it on the pavement?

The facts

* Toxocara canis – worms – are intestinal parasites which can cause sickness and diarrhoea in young animals but rarely affect adult animals.

* Toxocara canis infection has also been found in foxes, who are also regarded as sources of contamination. Adult dogs can ingest infective embryonated eggs from the soil or from other hosts such as rodents and birds.

* Humans can become infected with Toxocariasis if mature Toxocara (roundworm) eggs are swallowed. These eggs are sometimes present in grass, plants or soil where infected animals have defecated, or possibly from the faeces themselves.

* Studies have revealed that only 5% of adult pet dogs, and 15% of stray or kennelled dogs excrete Toxocara canis in their faeces.

* The chances of humans developing toxocariasis are minimal. It is estimated that there are only about two new cases of infection per million of the population each year (source, Pet Health Council, England).

* Children are most at risk, as they play in areas, such as grassland, where dog faeces are deposited. Children frequently put their hands in their mouths.

* On the rare occasions where human disease occurs, it usually causes only mild symptoms. Only in exceptional cases does it cause damage to an eye.

* Many surveys have been conducted throughout the world. Depending on the survey, between 0-27% of soil samples taken from public parks and private gardens contain Toxocara canis eggs. Strangely, these eggs have been found in soil samples from private gardens with no dogs!

* Tests show that some 2% of adults in the UK have Toxocara canis antibodies: they've been exposed to the eggs with no ill effects. The figure is not apparently higher for people who have regular contact with dogs, such as kennel workers.

* In warm weather conditions, it takes between two and three weeks before any eggs within faeces become infective; longer in cold weather. However, if the faeces are left to weather-down, the eggs can survive in the soil for up to three years.

* It's easy to worm your dog, it's effective, and it costs little. You can obtain worming tablets from your vet, or from the shops.

* Homoeopathic alternatives are available.

Nature's Way – An Alternative Approach to Healthcare

Herbalism

Recommendations

* Adult dogs should be wormed at least every six months.

* Pregnant bitches and those with young puppies should be wormed before mating, after the first 45 days of pregnancy, after giving birth, and whilst weaning puppies – consult your vet.

* Puppies should be wormed from two weeks of age, at least four times, until the puppy is at least six months old – because it's almost definite that your puppy is infected. Again, consult your vet to be effective and safe.

* Scoop as you go! Make friends, not enemies, of people who do not own dogs – share the joy!

* Take plastic bags in your pocket – you can safely scoop without touching anything unhygienic by using it like a roomy glove.

* Wash your hands before preparing food or eating, and after handling pets or gardening.

* Teach children to wash their hands before they eat; use wet wipes and tissues if soap and water are not to hand. Children should also be taught not to eat while playing, and not to eat soil, sand or grass.

* Park administrators can help by providing somewhere for dog owners to put the poop once they've scooped it.

So far, we have looked at the conventional veterinary approach to healing. But there are other ways in which your Golden can be helped towards a better, healthier life. The following case stories may surprise you.

Michael Brookman, who is owned by Harry the Golden Retriever, runs the Mendip Natural Healing Centre in England. The Centre specialises in herbalism, body harmony healing, counselling and iridology.

Harry has a very sensitive nature. He's a warm character who demonstrates his affection by bringing a gift to everyone he meets. During his first two years, Harry did not experience the best of health. He had problems with his anal glands; a cough which prompted the vet to suggest his tonsils be removed; a droopy eyelid which, again, the vet advised needed surgical attention; weeping eyes; and slight ear infections which distressed him and caused him to shake his head fairly frequently.

Harry

Homoeopathy

To a natural therapist like Michael, such 'little' problems are an indication that the general health needs immediate attention before the situation deteriorates. "I see the symptoms as an indication of imbalances at a deeper level," says Michael. "My tools for healing animals are herbs and a form of hands on healing called Body Harmony Healing."

Michael believes that the body has its own healing capacity which will always function, given the chance. Natural therapy works most effectively when we use it to work together with that innate capacity rather than from a concept of power or authority over the being that is in need of help.

Harry's first herbs in his daily diet were a standard powdered formulation called Kai Dog Tonic created by Michael. This is a combination of natural dried and powdered herbs which improve the overall function of the body to the extent that the body's own healing capacity is improved. Digestive, circulatory, urinary and nervous systems are supported.

Only a short while after starting to take the herbs, Harry became very ill – to the point where it appeared he might die. His usual vet was most concerned and put him on a short course of antibiotics. "He couldn't name the condition," said Michael, "but over a period of about three days, Harry became more and more listless. Feeling the stiffness in his prostrate body on the third day, it was as if he was already dead.

"Harry did manage to walk a little each day, very slowly, with his head held low and a look of absolute pain and dejection on his face. At the onset of this illness, I immediately prepared him special liquid herbs which were administered four times daily. Once a day he was given Body Harmony Healing which, in resting the hands very sensitively on various points of his body, gave support to that innate healing capacity within the body itself.

"Gradually, day by day, Harry continued on his recovery. We honestly felt that he didn't want to get better too quickly as he really enjoyed all the attention and fussing over him. In spite of this, Harry was vastly improved within two weeks – to the extent that he seemed healthier than he ever had before.

"He started to tear about the fields on his walks like a race horse, chasing deer and rabbits. He jumped up on large round bales of hay like a circus animal. Within a month of his illness, we felt confident enough to allow Harry to give up his liquid mixture and return to the standard herbal powder which we have continued to mix daily with his food."

Since his illness, Michael says that Harry has had no trouble with his anal glands; his eyes are clearer; his right eyelid has tightened up to equal the left one; his ears give less trouble, and the only time he croaks is when he is excitedly chasing an animal. "He's absolutely brimming with energy – a real handful, and I'm delighted!," Michael concludes.

Homoeopathy is a system of medicine which has been in worldwide use for over two hundred years. Whilst viewed with scepticism by many orthodox doctors and vets, it seems that more and more people are turning to it for help. Homoeopathic remedies are tested on people, not on animals.

Homoeopaths do not treat physical, emotional and mental or even spiritual illnesses separately, but regard them as connected. Remedies are prescribed on the basis of 'that which makes sick shall heal', or, 'treat like with like'. Accordingly, the substance which causes unwanted results if taken as an 'overdose', can also cure – stimulate the body's self healing powers – if taken in small doses. No-one really knows why it works, but there is abundant evidence to show it does. Our little Sophie is delighted to confirm that it did the job for her: she does so by romping around like a puppy and beaming with joy, when, before, arthritis made her give up on life.

History

At the age of seven, Sophie developed a pronounced limp. We gave her rest, keeping her in from walks for a few days, but the condition didn't improve. Several trips to the vet, and we were still none the wiser. The limp seemed to alternate between her two front paws. Was it her back? Her paws? Her shoulders or elbows?

Dogs can't talk – all we could tell was that Sophie was in pain, but we couldn't work out where the pain was coming from. The vet prescribed anti-inflamatories and pain killers, but Sophie's health continued to deteriorate.

The tablets were simply not helping. All our little darling wanted to do was lie in bed. We couldn't persuade her to accompany us on the early morning walk, and she growled testily at Samson if he dared to go near her. We were getting seriously worried.

We booked Sophie into the Cambridge Veterinary College, to discover that the problem lay in her paws. She was developing arthritis in the fourth digit of each front paw, probably caused by jumping off the 4ft wall which surrounds our garden.

We were offered two courses of action, the first being to continue with the tablets – the tablets which possibly stopped the pain but seemed to dope Sophie up to such an extent that she had no interest in life any more. The second alternative was to clip the offending nail right back so that she didn't walk on it, but placed her weight upon the three healthy 'fingers' on each paw.

Sophie was booked in for an operation, and came home minus the offending nails. Although we noticed a considerable improvement, Sophie still creaked noisily every time she stood up and seemed to be aging years before her time. If you didn't know otherwise, you would have thought Sophie was at least twelve.

Our first ray of hope came when we discovered Michael Brookman and his amazing Kai Dog Tonic. Michael believes that toxins accumulate in pockets around the body and it is this which causes arthritis. "What Sophie needs," he told me, "is something that will jump start her system."

The effects were astounding: energising. The next step, because she still limped from time to time, was to treat Sophie with Bryonia, a homeopathic remedy for arthritis. Not a day now goes by in which John and I do not marvel at the improvement in Sophie. She's a new girl, helped further by green lip mussel extract which can be purchased from health shops.

Because Homoeopathy treats the 'person' rather than the disease, different dogs (and people) need different remedies. Although Homoeopathy deals with a wide range of symptoms, the following preparations will help with arthritis. If these fail you, I strongly recommend you visit a homeopathic vet as only a small proportion of remedies can be purchased in the shops (usually chemists and health shops in England).

Bryonia is helpful where movement worsens the pain and relief is obtained by staying still.

Rhus Tox helps when muscle stiffness is improved by gentle movement.

Arnica is used where pain occurs following over-exertion.

Ruta is helpful when there is pain in tendons as well as muscles.

Improvement can usually be observed immediately. Occasionally the condition will deteriorate to begin with. This is usually a sign that the treatment is working so the dose should be stopped for around three days and resumed when the worsening has abated. Then the treatment is continued for three days, and then stopped. Sophie now has two Bryonia if she occasionally creaks.

Homoeopaths say that the remedies do not cause side effects because the body's energy is influenced rather than its chemical balance. It is therefore not possible to overdose, and the medicines are not intrinsically dangerous. However, they are clearly capable of stimulating the body's reactive forces powerfully, and should be treated with respect.

All homoeopathic medicines are available under the National Health Service in England, although it is unusual to find a doctor – or a vet – who has stumbled upon their benefits. See the appendix for further details.

Sweetie

Baking chocolate is toxic to your Golden. Sauces, gravies and desserts can cause serious digestive problems for your dog. Nuts cause problems because they are almost impossible for him to digest.

Chappie

Finally, Chappie's plight may both interest you, and give you hope.

You may remember that I described Chappie as a lugubrious dog . . . and we only discovered why when he was nine years old. Yet, for years, I just knew that something was wrong. What, after all, can a vet do when you tell him that your dog walks with his tail down? It doesn't exactly give him much to go on, does it?

And then, periodically, Chappie would go lame, limping about, unable to jump into the car; unable to walk upstairs. The vet would prescribe anti-inflammatories and two weeks' rest. The condition would clear, only to recur several months later - and the anti-inflammatories were back, together with the enforced rest.

As he got older, the problem worsened. We were told that Chappie had hip dysplasia but that, at his age, pain killers were really the only solution. Yet the tablets may have been killing the pain, but they hadn't retrieved any quality of life for Chappie. I couldn't bear to see Chappie suffer so much, and asked to be referred to an holistic vet. The opposition was so fierce that we decided to move to another practice.

Once again, Chappie went through a barrage of X-rays and we discovered that he didn't have hip dysplasia after all, he had two ruptured cruciate ligaments which - guess what - could only be treated with pain killers at his age. We had to accept the fact that Chappie would never be able to walk properly again. Well, stroppy is my middle name, and I wasn't prepared to accept that. Our new vet agreed to refer us to Christopher Day, the holistic vet, and the magic started working.

Three respected and caring alternative practitioners have worked together for the common good. Dana Green, a McTimoney Chiropractor, discovered that one of Chappie's hips was about an inch further forward than the other, and that his back had curved to compensate. She put him right. Christopher Day treated Chappie with acupuncture and homoeopathy, telling us that the body possesses an innate ability to heal itself, given the correct help.

Our orthodox vet had told me that a ruptured cruciate ligament is a ruptured cruciate ligament: it can't grow back (just like a piece of string can't join itself together once you've cut it in half).

Now then . . . after about two months' treatment under Mr Day, Chappie was game for two walks a day. Before, we had a dog who could barely walk, who refused to come out on walks, whose back curved in an effort to place all his weight on his front feet, and who, we believed, would have had a most pitiful end to his life. Thanks to Mr Day, Chappie had taken to sitting and barking with glee, just to tell us how happy he was. There was a light shining in his eyes that wasn't there before.

So far, so good . . . Mr Day then began to work in conjunction with Chrissie Mason PhD, a radionics expert. Radionics is a fascinating subject. It takes a fair bit of lateral thinking to get your brain round it, and an open mind. To effect a cranial gear change, imagine that illnesses are created first in the mind: you are what you think (how else

Chappie

98

can stress - mental anxiety - cause ulcers, eczema or asthma?).

There's a bigger picture, too. Chrissie Mason told me that within the universe, both organic and inorganic matter are unified by invisible forces and energies.

"Animals comprise of almost identical organ functions as humans," Chrissie said. "And these are made up of compounds of matter and further complex compounds to create the physical form. Each animal is unique, and has a general structure that regenerates, similar to the human form.

"The emotions, sensations and feelings influence the cellular metabolism of all animals and can bring about disharmony and disease. Dietary aspects can also cause reactions within the physical body."

In orthodox veterinary medicine, the practitioner will use an X-ray procedure and the unseen rays will pass through the organs and record their deviations on a photographic plate. Similarly, with the help of instruments, the radionics practitioner measures the unseen electro-magnetic fields and the already existing deviations, and she records these measurements as they differ from normality.

Using a lock of Chappie's hair (as with DNA theory, the cell structure follows the same pattern throughout the body, so hair can act as a 'witness'), Chrissie conducted an analysis and offered the following comments:

"Chappie has experienced a trauma of a violent nature at some point in his life, and the residues of this trauma are embedded within the cell memory. Not much is wrong with Chappie's skeletal system, the primary malady rests in the fault of biochemistry. This has a direct affect on the muscles and especially the myelin sheaths.

"It appears that Chappie has an imbalance of iron molecules in his body, causing a relaxation and general lack of tone within his muscular fibres. Chappie's liver is congested, and there is evidence of a general lack of protein. There would also be a general poor assimilation of nutrients from the diet. It is possible that Chappie has been exposed to heavy metal toxicity, particularly lead."

Well!

The remedies, in conjunction with Chris Day's prescribed homoeopathic Pedaflo and acupuncture, consist of a mineral supplement to aid iron absorption and to assist cellular metabolism. Secondly, Chappie was prescribed homoeopathic remedies Ferrum Phos. and Plumbum Met. John and I have supplemented this with green lip mussel extract which is said to aid movement (and is certainly missed by Chappie if we stop giving it to him).

The results

Chris Day and Chrissie Mason gave us the very best Christmas present we could ask for. The present? Chappie started to get up to greet guests as they arrived at the front door; and he was up to his first longish walk on Christmas morning. Our Chappie returned to the house brimming with delight, energy, and self satisfaction.

As the months roll on, we see improvements in Chappie every day. More recently, we took the dogs to the seaside . . . I couldn't believe it, I repeat, I just couldn't believe it, when Chappie decided to jump down from a six foot sand dune and promptly charged off to persecute rabbits. We have our hooligan back again!

So, call alternative treatments mumbo jumbo if you like. All we know is that they have helped Chappie and Sophie enormously. Unless a dog understands a lot more than we give them credit for, their successful treatments can't possibly be the result of the 'placebo' effect.

Please note, in England it is currently illegal to have an animal treated by any practitioner who is not a qualified vet, unless referred by a vet. Even where the holistic vet is also a conventionally qualified vet, as with Chris Day, professional courtesy usually demands that the animal's 'regular' vet refers the animal.

In any event, I would advise you talk to your orthodox vet first, but I would also say that, where conventional veterinary practice may fail, alternatives have been known to work wonders. Perhaps we need a few cynical orthodox vets to conduct some serious research?

Coming from the right family

Like most people with Irish forebears, I am a direct descendant of Brian Boru, the greatest king of Ireland – or that's what my father would tell you! He's got a certificate to prove it – although I suspect we're really commoners after all.

You can imagine my delight, then, when I read about Champion Camrose Nicholas of Westley in Joan Gill's book. "He really does smile," wrote Joan, "by drawing back his mouth and screwing up his eyes." I rushed off to take a look at my smiling Sophie's pedigree, and there it was: Sophie is a direct descendant of the great Camrose Nicholas of Westley: fact. Blue-blooded by association is good enough for me!

It is, of course, the dog show which enables people like me, with no particular claim to fame, to bask in the glory of our precious pets' noble forebears. In the show ring, the pursuit of excellence is everything; lineage is almost all. Dedication, attention to detail, years of selective breeding, time, toil and tenacity – these are the ingredients which produce champions. Showing, quite definitely, is not for the slapdash or the half-hearted, as my own experience demonstrates:

Well, we were disgusted! Off we trotted – Chappie, Sophie, Prudence and Samson – to the local exemption show, expecting to come home laden with trophies and rosettes, and what did we come home with? Zippo! My beautiful, silky, gorgeous and recently bathed four were overlooked, discarded and rejected. Was the judge *blind?*

But, of course, to get to the top you've got to start off with a quality dog, and then you've got to know how to move your darling to best advantage. You need to know how to walk him and stand him; how to groom him and keep him in tip top condition. Importantly, you've got to enjoy it, and so has your precocious pooch.

Ringcraft classes help. Here your Golden will get used to being amongst other dogs: he will learn how to mind his own business and not say hello to the other canines. He will get used to standing so that the judge can have a good look, feel his bone structure and examine his teeth. You will learn how to move in the ring so that his lovely lithe body looks like a dog food commercial. And you will learn which bits need to be trimmed.

Ron Bradbury started the second ringcraft class in the UK, many years ago. He is now one of the country's most respected judges (as well as the owner of the late acclaimed Champion Nortonwood Faunus and a whole host of other notable champions). Mr Bradbury says: "It's easier to judge a well-behaved dog than a bad one. It's hard work judging a dog that doesn't stand for you or let you see his teeth; you can't see all the good points.

"Quality stands out," he says. "A lot of quality is hereditary. Better quality always comes from a linebred dog. For instance, Champion Jobeka Jasper of Nortonwood is linebred back to Nortonwood Faunus. Three of his four grandparents come through Faunus: he's virtually a reincarnation of Faunus."

The Life of a Show Golden

(In-breeding is used by breeders to emphasise a desirable quality, but sometimes also emphasises undesirable qualities. Here, it is not uncommon to mate a father with its daughter, or a brother with its sister. With line breeding, on the other hand, the dogs are related, but not so closely. Out-crossing is mating two unrelated dogs: whilst the parents' attributes may be well known, the characteristics of resulting offspring are unpredictable.)

Showmanship also helps in the ring. "I remember one Flat Coated Retriever that won Best in Show at Crufts," says Mr Bradbury. "You would think that Best in Show at Crufts would be without faults. But she could have been a little bit bigger all round, yet she's such an extrovert and so beautifully balanced. The crowd loved her because she moved like a train – it's all part of showmanship at that level. It's like stars on the stage, the crowd makes them."

Madge Bradbury judges Golden Retrievers at championship shows. She says: "You need lots of patience and kindness to succeed in the ring. I hate to see people getting cross with their dogs, and especially if it's a puppy. It's better to let puppy be naughty and try to get the best out of it rather than struggle with it.

"It's also possible to overdo the ringcraft classes. Ringcraft is good to a certain point, but if you go with a young puppy week after week, you end up with a dog that stands perfectly but is bored stiff. It's lovely to see a happy puppy in the show ring: one who plays its owner up a little bit rather than one who just creeps along with boredom."

Being a show Golden is a bit like being a famous model: you shouldn't eat titbits, and you have to exercise. Some show dogs are kept on the lead because they have to remain in tiptop condition: charging through brambles or thick undergrowth before a show is a definite no-no.

You have to be brushed and washed; your nails need clipping. You have to practice your pose and have your teeth cleaned. You need to be an extrovert and come alive in a crowd. And you need to wait patiently in the wings until it's your turn centre stage.

For the humans, showing can be great fun so long as you don't take it too seriously or, if you do, so long as you have a truly remarkable dog. It's also a great way to make friends and, if you intend to breed, it enables you to prove your canine's credentials.

The Standard

There are many devoted people around the world who take care to ensure that a Golden Retriever remains a Golden Retriever. These hard-working people are breeding-in the positive attributes of the breed and trying to remove faults. It is this, after all, that makes a particular breed what it is.

A perfect Golden Retriever comes close to the 'standards' on the following pages.

USA

General appearance:

A symmetrical, powerful, active dog, sound and well put together, not clumsy nor long in the leg, displaying a kindly expression and possessing a personality that is eager, alert and self-confident. Primarily a hunting dog, he should be shown in hard working condition. Overall appearance, balance, gait and purpose to be given more emphasis than any of his component parts.

Head:

Broad in skull, slightly arched laterally and longitudinally without prominence of frontal bones (forehead) or occipital bones. Stop well defined but not abrupt. Foreface deep and wide, nearly as long as skull. Muzzle straight in profile, blending smoothly and strongly into skull; when viewed in profile or from above, slightly deeper and wider at stop than at tip. No heaviness in flews. Removal of whiskers is permitted but not preferred.

Eyes:

Friendly and intelligent in expression, medium large with dark, close-fitting rims, set well apart and reasonably deep in sockets. Colour preferably dark brown; medium brown acceptable. Slant eyes and narrow, triangular eyes detract from correct expression and are to be faulted. No white or haw visible when looking straight ahead. Dogs showing evidence of functional abnormality of eyelids or eyelashes (such as, but not limited to, trichiasis, entropion, ectropion, or distichiasis) are to be excused from the ring.

Teeth:

Scissors bite, in which the outer side of the lower incisors touches the inner side of the upper incisors. Undershot or overshot bite is a disqualification. Misalignment of teeth (irregular placement of incisors) or level bite (incisors meet each other edge to edge) is undesirable, but not to be confused with undershot or overshot. Full dentition. Obvious gaps are serious faults.

United Kingdom

General appearance:

Should be a symmetrical active powerful dog, a good level mover, sound and well put together, with kindly expression, not clumsy, nor long in the leg.

Head and skull:

Broad skull, well set on and a clean muscular neck, muzzle, powerful and wide, not weak-jawed, good stop.

Eyes:

Dark and well set apart, very kindly expression, with dark rims.

Mouth:

Teeth should be sound and strong, Neither overshot nor undershot, the lower teeth just behind but just touching the upper teeth.

USA

Nose:
Black or brownish black, though fading to a lighter shade in cold weather is not serious. Pink nose or one seriously lacking in pigmentation to be faulted.

Ears:
Rather short with front edge attached well behind and just above the eye and falling close to cheek. When pulled forward, the tip of the ear should just cover the eye. Low, hound-like ear set to be faulted.

Neck:
Medium long, merging gradually into well laid back shoulders, giving sturdy, muscular appearance. Untrimmed natural ruff. No throatiness.

Body:
Well-balanced, short coupled, deep through the chest. Chest between forelegs at least as wide as a man's closed hand including thumb, with well developed forechest. Brisket extends to elbow. Ribs long and well sprung but not barrel shaped, extending well towards hindquarters. Loin short, muscular, wide and deep, with very little tuck-up. Back line strong and level from withers to slightly sloping croup, whether standing or moving. Slabsidedness, narrow chest, lack of depth in brisket, sloping back line, roach or sway back, excessive tuck-up, flat or steep croup to be faulted.

Forequarters:
Muscular, well co-ordinated with hind quarters capable of free movement. Shoulder blades long and well laid back with upper tips fairly close together at withers. Upper arms appear about the same length as the blades, close to the ribs without looseness. Legs, viewed from the front, straight with good bone, but not to the point of coarseness. Pasterns short and strong, sloping slightly with no suggestion of weakness.

Hindquarters:
Broad and strongly muscled. Profile of croup slopes slightly; the pelvic bone slopes at a slightly greater angle (approximately 30 degrees from horizontal). In a natural stance, the femur joins the pelvis at approximately a 90 degree angle; stifles well bent; hocks well let down with short strong rear pasterns. Legs straight when viewed from the rear. Cow hocks, spread hocks and stickle hocks to be faulted.

Feet:
Medium size, round, compact, and well knuckled, with thick pads. Excess hair may be trimmed to show natural size and contour. Dewclaws on forelegs may be removed, but are normally left on. Splayed or hare feet to be faulted.

United Kingdom

Ears:
Well proportioned, of moderate size, and well set on.

Neck:
The neck should be clean and muscular.

Body:
Well-balanced, short coupled, and deep through the heart. Ribs deep and well sprung.

Forequarters:
The forelegs should be straight with good bone. Shoulders should be well laid back and long in the blade.

Hindquarters:
The loins and legs should be strong and muscular, with good second thighs and well bent stifles. Hocks well let down, not cow-hocked.

Feet:
Round and cat-like, not open or splayed.

USA

Tail:

Well set on, thick and muscular at the base, following the natural line of the croup. Tail bones extend to, but not below, the point of hock. Carried with merry action, level or with some moderate upward curve; never curled over back nor between legs.

Coat:

Dense and water repellent with good undercoat. Outer coat firm and resilient, neither coarse nor silky, lying close to body; may be straight or wavy. Moderate feathering on back of forelegs and underbody; heavier feathering on front of neck, back of thighs and underside of tail. Coat on head, paws, and front of legs is short and even. Excessive length, open coats, and limp, soft coats are very undesirable. Feet may be trimmed and stray hairs neatened, but the natural appearance of coat and outline should not be altered by cutting or clipping.

Color:

Rich lustrous golden of various shades. Feathering may be lighter than rest of coat. With the exception of greying or whitening of face or body due to age, any white marking, other than a few white hairs on the chest, should be penalised according to its extent. Allowable light shadings are not to be confused with white markings. Predominant body color which is either extremely pale or extremely dark is undesirable. Some latitude should be given to the light puppy whose coloring shows promise of deepening with maturity. Any noticeable area of black or other off-color hair is a serious fault.

Gait:

When trotting, gait is free, smooth, powerful, and well co-ordinated, showing good reach. Viewed from any position, legs turn neither in nor out, nor do feet cross or interfere with each other. As speed increases, feet tend to converge toward center line of balance. It is recommended that dogs be shown on a loose lead to reflect true gait.

Size:

Males 23"-24" in height at withers; females 21.5"-22.5." Dogs up to one inch above or below standard size should be proportionately penalised. Deviation in height of more than one inch from the standard shall disqualify. Length from breastbone to point of buttocks slightly greater than height at withers in ratio of 12:11. Weight for dogs 65-75lbs; bitches 55-65lbs.

United Kingdom

Tail:

Should not be carried too gay nor curled at the tip.

Coat:

Should be flat or wavy with good feathering, and dense water repellent undercoat.

Colour:

Any shade of gold or cream but neither red nor mahogany. The presence of a few white hairs on the chest is permissible. White collar, feet, toes, or blase should be penalised. Nose should be black.

Weight and size:

The average weight in good hard condition should be: dogs 32-37kg (70-80lbs); bitches 27-32kg (60-70lbs). Height at shoulder: dogs 56-61cm (22-24"); bitches 51-56cm (20-22").

USA

Temperament:

Friendly, reliable, and trustworthy. Quarrelsomeness or hostility towards other dogs or people in normal situations, or an unwarranted show of timidity or nervousness, is not in keeping with Golden Retriever character. Such actions should be penalised according to their significance.

Disqualifications:

1. Deviation in height of more than one inch from standard either way. 2. Undershot or overshot bite.

Faults:

Any departure from the described ideal shall be considered faulty to the degree to which it interferes with the breed's purpose or is contrary to breed character.

100>

A good American specimen: Jazz, owner Brenda Surack

101

Three good British specimens - although many British Goldens are darker

Well, once you've worked out what stop, trichiasis, throatiness, brisket, croup, slabsidedness and pasterns mean, you can begin to evaluate whether your Golden is a good specimen for the show ring or not. Alternatively, you could speak to someone who has been evaluating the breed for years, and who can take one look at your friend and tell you whether he has a chance or not. The person who bred your puppy might be a good start, or she can recommend a top breeder to you.

The standard is complex; different judges have different opinions . . . and what is 'angulation' anyway? (Angulation is the angle of the bones in relation to one-another. For example, 'shoulder blades well laid back with upper tips fairly close together at withers'. Umm.)

The American versus the British Golden Retriever

Should you compare an English show champion with an American champion you would be forgiven for thinking that the two dogs were entirely different, if related, breeds.

On the whole, perfect British show Goldens are 'chunkier' than their American counterparts with broader heads, and it is acceptable for their coats to be much lighter in colour. Many Americans abhor the English Golden Retriever.

In contrast, certain English aficionados might claim that the American show Golden has too narrow a head, too pointy a nose; and the coat is often too red. It seems to me that the American Golden is more similar to the English working strain. I understand that American Goldens differ in temperament: they are more active than their English cousins, exhibiting the speedy characteristics of the Welsh Border Collie, whereas English show Goldens are acknowledged as being less biddable than English working Goldens.

(Americans seem, in the language of dangerous generalisations, to be much more competitive than the British. It makes sense, then, that their favourite canine should possess the attributes which make winning in competitive sports a distinct possibility. Also, I have found that a great number of American Golden lovers actively participate in sports with their dogs, whereas we English primarily seem to seek companionship. Please note, however, that I have found that both nationalities share an equal measure of passionate love for their dogs. I'd also like to make it clear that I have no personal input in this – before I get beaten over the head. All I care about is the temperament, and the temperament should be friendly.)

102

Razz at 16 months having just won BOB. (Purban Razzle Dazzle)

Shows in England

Exemption Show

This is the Brit's entry into the world of showing. Exemption shows are the fun end of it all and could include categories such as dog with the waggiest tail, dog with the happiest smile, dog the judge would most like to take home, and so on. Classes tend to be broad. There might, for example, be a working dog class, a non-working dog class, a puppy class, a veteran class, an open class, and others. Exemption shows are usually organised in conjunction with village fetes or fund raising events.

Sanction Show

To enter a sanction show, your Golden must be registered with the Kennel Club, and you must be a member of the organisation promoting the show. Challenge Certificate winners may not enter; nor can dogs who have won five or more first prizes in post-graduate or higher classes.

Limited Show

Again, your Golden must be registered with the Kennel Club, and you must be a member of the organisation promoting the show. Only Challenge Certificate winners are barred.

Open Show

Any dog who is registered with the Kennel Club may enter an open show. The open show is the beginning of the 'big time', although novices are encouraged to enter their dogs, and young dogs are also welcomed. Money prizes are on offer, and points can be won here for a Junior Warrant title. (A Junior Warrant is awarded if the dog wins twenty-five points in breed classes at open and championship shows before reaching the age of eighteen months.)

Championship Show

Challenge Certificates (CCs) can be won at the championship show, and three CCs do a Show Champion make. Having said that, it is incredibly difficult to obtain a CC. First, the dog must win his or her individual class, and then he must compete in and win a class in which all other class winners are shown. To become a Champion (without the 'Show' prefix), the Golden must have earned a Qualifying Certificate (working dog certificate), or he must have won a prize at a field trial.

To become a Dual Champion, a dog must become both a show Champion and a Field Trial Champion. To become a Field Trial Champion, he needs to win two first prizes at two different Field Trials in the Open or All-age stakes for Retrievers, or the Retriever Championship stake. Dual championship is no easy feat.

Shows in America

Match Show

The Match Show is the ideal place for novices to start in the USA. Relatively inexpensive to enter, the Match Show will give you a good idea as to how your dog will perform in the ring, and tell you whether you need to work harder at your own presentational skills. Judges are often happy to help new exhibitors by answering questions and offering advice about dogs and how to handle them.

Point Shows

There are two types of 'point' shows in America: the All Breed Show, and the Independent Specialty Show. Dogs become Champions when they win enough points, detailed later.

Puppies between the ages of six and nine months, and born in the USA, are eligible to enter the *puppy class* at any point show. Some shows have a second class for puppies between nine and twelve months of age.

The *novice class* is for dogs of six months and older who were born in America or Canada, and who have not won three first prizes in the novice class, a first prize in any class other than puppy, or one or more points towards a championship. He is allowed to have won any number of prizes in the puppy class to compete in the novice class.

The *bred-by-exhibitor* class is for dogs born in the USA (or Canada if registered with the Kennel Club of Canada), who are six months of age or older, not champions, and entered by the owner or a member of the owner's immediate family. The dog must also have been bred by the person showing the dog.

The *American-bred* class is for dogs who were conceived and born in the United States.

The *open class* is for dogs aged six months or older. There are no further restrictions. Entry is usually large, so competition is stiff.

The *winners' class* consists of all the first placed dogs from the previous classes (Puppy, Novice, BBE, American Bred and Open). The best dog (theoretically) from that group is selected as Winner's Dog and earns points. The dog that is placed second in the class from which the Winner's dog came (usually, but not always, Open) then joins the remaining first place finishers in the rings. The best of these is then chosen as Reserve Winner's Dog. The process is repeated for the bitches. The Winner's Dog and Winner's Bitch then join the dogs entered specifically in the Best of Breed class.

The dog selected as *Best of Breed* does not win championship points. They are won in the Winner's class. After a Best of Breed is selected, there is then selected a Best of Opposite Sex (this being the best dog or bitch that is the opposite sex to the Best of Breed) and then a Best of Winners is also selected from the Winner's Dog and Winner's Bitch. Thus, a dog can very rarely be Winner's Dog (or Bitch) and Best of Breed and Best of Winners all at once! Confused? Believe me, this is the simplified version!

Point System

Points – from one to five – are awarded to the winner, depending upon the number of dogs of the same sex he or she had to beat in order to win. There might, for example, be fewer than half-a-dozen or so competitors to win one point, going up to around fifty defeated competitors to be awarded five points. The scale of points is agreed by the American Kennel Club annually.

Three-, four- or five-point wins are called 'majors'. A dog must have won two majors under two different judges and have received at least one point from a third judge to become a *Champion*. In addition, the dog must have accrued a total of fifteen points from all its wins.

A dog can also gain points by winning the sporting group class. If he wins this, he is required to compete in the best in show competition. Best in show is not available at a Specialty show.

Veteran classes, Field Trial classes, and Sweepstake classes (a class with a 'fresh' judge) are also often held at All-Breed and Specialty shows.

Equipment

It's no good thinking, as I did, that you can give your dog a brush, stroll along to a show and come away with all the prizes. Lots of people take showing seriously, and they have all the kit in their bags to help them win. They have crates to transport their dogs in and provide somewhere warm and secure while waiting in the wings. They have grooming tables, tack boxes, brushes, combs, scissors, nail cutters, first aid kits, towels, water sprayers, packed lunches, foldable seats, mobile exercise pens, iced water . . . the list is seemingly endless, although not obligatory.

The show calendar is also pretty full. If you mean serious business, then be prepared to travel to a show most weekends. Good luck!

J. LOBBAN

103

Field Trials

The following information provides only a brief outline of this vast subject, which demands a book (or two) in its own right.

When Lord Tweedmouth first bred the Golden Retriever, his plan was to produce the perfect working gun dog. Soft and gentle they may be, but Golden Retrievers are genetically hunters. But to be good hunters, in partnership with humans, they must also be 'biddable'.

Trials are judged on steadiness, soft mouths, marking and hunting ability, nose, biddability, speed, style, using the wind, collecting runners (wounded birds), and being able to direct the dog to a blind retrieve. It is important that the dog responds quickly to the whistle and takes direction from hand signals.

Trials are held during the shooting season, between October and January each year. In working tests, canvas dummies are used for retrieving, so it is similar to the work required of a Retriever out on a shoot. Even if you don't like the idea of shooting game, the use of dummies enables you to enjoy the sport.

Field Trials and Working Tests in the UK

There are four types of Field Trial for Retrievers the United Kingdom, as defined by the Kennel Club:

1. OPEN – a Stake in which dogs have the opportunity of gaining a qualification towards the title of Field Trial Champion or towards entry in the Championships or Champion Stake for its breed and in which entry is open to all dogs of a specified breed or breeds; it may be limited to a prescribed number of runners, in which case these shall be decided by a draw conducted in accordance with Regulation 6g (so that preference is given to previous performance).

2. ALL-AGED – a Stake which is open to all dogs of a specified breed or breeds without restriction as to their age, but which may be restricted by any other conditions which may be determined by the Society.

3. NOVICE – a Stake which is confined to dogs which have not gained the following awards:

Retrievers: First, Second or Third in Open Stakes; or

First in an All-Aged or Novice Stake.

4. PUPPY– a Stake which is confined to dogs whelped not earlier than 1st January in the year preceding the date of the Field Trials. (For such Stakes run in January, a dog which was a puppy in the previous year shall be deemed to be still a puppy.)

There are two parts to a shoot proper, the walk-up and the drive. In the walk-up, the judges, handlers, dogs, guns, beaters and number carriers walk in a line. The game is flushed close to the line and shot. The judge picks a dog to make a retrieve. If the chosen dog fails to retrieve the game, a second dog will be called to pick up. If two birds have been shot at the same time, the handler is asked to get his dog to pick up a specific bird.

In the drive, the handlers and dogs form into a crescent-shaped line. Beaters go through the field and drive the game towards the guns, and the shooting begins. When the shooting is over the dogs are requested to make retrieves, some of which may be over water.

To become a Champion (as opposed to a Show Champion) in the United Kingdom, a Golden must have obtained three Challenge Certificates at Championship Shows under three different judges, and have obtained a Show Gundog Working Certificate. To win this, the dog must show that he is not gun-shy, hunts and retrieves tenderly to hand, and enters water when requested to do so.

Field Trial work is quite different in the United States, being much more water based. The American emphasis seems to be placed upon identical chances, so that the test is as equal as possible for all dogs. The game tends to be planted, or released from crates and then shot. In England the pleasure lies in partaking in a natural sport where the game is freshly shot, and luck plays a greater part.

"Great importance is placed upon collecting wounded birds as quickly as possible in the UK," says Joan Gill. "Watching a dog taking the line on a runner that has gone a long way is extremely exciting. This is where the dog with a really good nose excels. When I saw a trial in the USA, however, I noticed that they didn't send the competitors for any birds that ran, presumably to try to make the test equal."

There are four stakes: The Open All-Age is open to dogs over six months of age and carries Championship points. The Amateur All-Age is for dogs over six months of age and carries Amateur Championship points. The Qualifying stake is open to all dogs over six months, but carries no Championship points. Finally, the Derby Stake is open to dogs between six months of age and two years. Most licensed trials run for three days.

104

Jiggs - owned by Mike Carlucci

Tracking

For a dog to become a Field Champion in America, he or she must have won one All-Breed Trial Open, a Limited or Special All-Age Stake, plus five additional points.

Mike and Jackie Grubb report that field trials in the US have become very difficult. "In order to succeed," says Mike, "you have to use a professional trainer and have a dog that is trained very mechanically, almost to the point of being a robot. A common test in the qualifying test (only the second level) might be two marks and a water blind. In the upper classes, a five bird test (triple mark and two blinds) is not uncommon. There is much handling and whistle blowing."

Tracking is an extremely popular sport in the United States and Canada, but it is still a minority sport in the United Kingdom. In fact, I have been unable to find anyone who knows of Golden Retrievers used for tracking in the UK – which will surprise most Americans. Bloodhounds are used in the UK for hunting which involves following a human scent, off the lead, for up to six miles. Tracking, as described here, is mainly confined to German Shepherds, or Alsatians, in the UK.

The American Kennel Club states that, "The purpose of a Tracking Test is to demonstrate the dog's ability to recognize and follow human scent, a skill that is useful in the service of mankind.

"Tracking, by nature, is a vigorous, noncompetitive outdoor sport. Tracking Tests demonstrate the willingness and enjoyment of the dog in its work, and should always represent the best in sportsmanship and camaraderie by the people involved."

The following information is taken from the American Kennel Club Tracking Regulations, effective from July 1, 1990.

105

Jazz - owned by Brenda Surack

A dog wears a harness while tracking, and the handler follows the dog at a distance of more than 20ft using a leash which is between 20 and 40 feet in length. Each dog follows a unique track, but each track is designed to be of equal complexity. Before the test, a tracklayer walks along a route which has been marked with flags the day before by the judges.

He or she carries personal articles which are of a similar size to a glove or a wallet so that the items are impregnated with his or her scent. These are then dropped along the course, one article being used for the Tracking Dog Test, and four articles for the Tracking Dog Excellent Test.

The tracklayer is asked to walk naturally and pause at each flag. He picks up all but the first two flags in a Tracking Test/TD, or all but the first flag and the crosstrack flags in the Tracking Test/TDX. The dropped articles should not be visible from a distance of more than 20 feet, or covered or concealed in any way.

107

Magic - owned by Sarah Brinegar

Handlers may give verbal commands and verbal encouragement to the dog, but they may not use commands, signals or body movements to indicate the location or direction of the track. A commendable rule is that handlers are not allowed to use harsh verbal commands or physical force to discipline the dog.

Tracking Test/TD

Dogs entering a Tracking Test/TD (TD stands for Tracking Dog) must first receive certification (a written statement from an approved person that the dog has satisfactorily completed a test of equivalent complexity to the actual Tracking Test/TD).

Track requirements are, in simplified form:

1. The track is between 440 and 500 yards.

2. Each leg of the track is at least 50 yards.

3. The scent on the track is between 30 minutes and two hours old.

4. Between three and five left and right turns are used.

5. There should be more than two right angle turns, and at least two of these should be in the open where there are no fences or boundaries to guide the dog.

6. No part of the track must follow within 15 yards of any fence or boundary.

7. No part of a track should be within 50 yards of any other part of the same track.

106

Bear - owned by Susan Rezy

133

8. Consecutive parallel tracks should not be used.

9. No part of any track should be laid within 75 yards of another track, but if two tracks go in opposite directions from the same area, the starting flags can be as close as 50 yards to each other.

10. A track should not cross water or a paved road. No TD track should have changes of cover that would be suitable for a TDX obstacle.

Tracking Test/TDX

The Tracking Test/TDX is designed to show unquestionably that the dog has the ability to discriminate scent and possesses the stamina, perseverance and courage to do so under a wide variety of conditions. This Test presents difficult challenges. Only about 20 per cent of those dogs trying to earn this title have succeeded.

Dogs may be entered into the Tracking Test/TDX (TDX stands for Tracking Dog Excellent) once they have earned the TD title. The TDX test differs from the TD test in the following ways:

1. The course is longer: between 800 and 1000 yards.

2. The scent on the track is older: between three and five hours old.

3. More turns – between five and seven – are used.

4. Cross-tracks are laid. Here, an hour and 15 minutes to an hour and 45 minutes after the original track is laid, two people walk a course crossing the track at two points. (This course is marked-out with flags by the judges and the crosstrackers remove the flags as they go.) The cross track crosses the original track at right angles but must keep a specified distance away from articles, obstacles or turns on the actual track. A dog that follows a cross-track for more than 50 yards is failed.

5. The course has at least two obstacles to test the dog's ability to adapt to changing scent conditions; the dog's ability to continue scenting while overcoming physical obstacles; and the dog's ability to continue scenting under difficult and varied handling conditions. They include various types of terrain and cover including woods and vegetation. Natural obstacles such as a stream, or man-made obstacles such as fences or bridges, may be used.

6. Four articles are dropped by the tracklayer, at points designated by the judges.

7. Since there is no second starting flag, the handler must wait for the dog to commit itself before leaving the starting flag.

8. The dog can be physically assisted by the handler when obstacles, barriers, or terrain so require.

Canadian tracking is very similar in format as to length and aging. The main differences in the TDX test include the use of just one cross-tracker; no article is left at the starting stake as in the United States; and one of the first two articles may be missed.

Gongs

TD is a Tracking Dog

TDX is a Tracking Dog Excellent

CD is a Companion Dog

UCD is the United Kennel Club Companion Dog Title

WC is a Working Certificate

I firmly believe that when you share your life with a Golden Retriever, you embark upon a journey of spiritual discovery. We are fortunate that, faultlessly generous and tolerant, most Goldens put up with our mistakes, accept us when we get it wrong, and somehow manage to end up well-behaved and well-adjusted despite all our efforts. Our friends give us the opportunity, and the second chances, to strive for understanding.

It seems to me that you can no more own an animal than you can own God's earth. We can be responsible for them, look after them, share their joy – but we rely, always, upon their willing co-operation.

We have been fed a lot of nonsense about dog training over the years – much of it well meaning, but much of it sadly misguided. We've been told to rub our dogs' noses in it if they make a mess in the house. We've been instructed to hit them on the nose with rolled up newspapers. We've been advised to establish dominance by beating them into submission. Anyone who has a Golden need only look at the reaction to see how wrong this advice patently is.

Is this any way to treat any living being – and does it actually work? Do we, after all, want to bring animals into our homes in order to assert our own macho images and make ourselves, and our canine friends, miserable in the process? Of course we don't – or we shouldn't.

As the Hindu mystics say: "Treat each man as your honoured guest." I am extending this philosophy to: "Treat each living creature as your honoured guest." (Un-invited guests such as cockroaches and fleas shall be asked politely to leave!)

This chapter on training is based upon the belief that most animals will do most things you ask of them if you ask in a positive way. It is based upon the belief that they deserve our respect, not overbearing power. And it is based upon kindness and mutual co-operation, not brute force. I'm not talking indulgence here, I'm talking partnership.

Forget all you have been taught about training for a moment – all the choke chains, the yanking and the pulling – and engage the lateral thinking part of your intellect.

You will discover that it is possible to train a Golden Retriever using the whiplash of *the reward*, the stick of *fun* and the coercion of *love and affection*. It is the art of thinking and acting positive. Scientists and academics have studied animal behaviour in great depth and have concluded that you don't need to force an animal to obey your commands.

The greater part of the credit for this chapter must go to Erica Peachey, one such scientist, who has unselfishly devoted a great deal of her time, and taken a great deal of trouble, to 'put me right' and crystallise my vague beliefs.

Erica Peachey graduated from Hull University with a BSc (Hons) in Psychology, specialising in animal behaviour. She then spent time at the Royal School of Veterinary Studies, Edinburgh, and later worked with one of the United Kingdom's foremost animal behaviourists. Today, Erica runs her own animal behaviour practice in the North of England.

These training concepts have evolved from my own experience (trial and error), and discussions with Erica who, in common with her colleagues within the Association of Pet Behaviour Counsellors, has the experience to know that 'soft and gentle overcomes harsh and strong'.

Also, in the process of writing this book, I have had the pleasure of speaking to a good number of Golden Retriever 'nuts': people like me who love the breed. Graham Hall of the famous Stirchley kennels sums it up when he says that typical Golden owners are gentle, quiet people who are attracted by the breed's gentle, quiet reputation – so I know you won't have too much trouble experimenting with this approach and seeing that it works.

The gentle art of seduction

109

Note:

It must be noted that the following 'tips' are directed at the average human living with an average Golden. Very occasionally you come across a Golden who breaks the stereotypical image – either due to biological factors or to deeply embedded behavioural problems. Whilst the vast majority of Golden Retrievers are gentle, biddable and even-tempered, there are exceptions. If you experience severe problems with your Golden, consult your vet who can refer you to a qualified animal behaviourist.

Please also note that the following tips assume that you are starting with a clean slate: a young puppy. If you have an older dog, then take a look at the section specially devoted to training a Golden Oldie.

110

Joanna, Prudence and Chappie strut their stuff

The basic well-behaved Golden

Originally, I wrote that 'only a percentage of Golden owners have the time or the inclination to train their friends up to the highest standards of obedience'. For most of us, I said, 'the ability to live in peaceful co-existence with one-another and our neighbours is all we ask'. I had forgotten, of course, that I have devoted many minutes, hours, days and years to bring my four into a state of near 'peaceful co-existence'.

Erica Peachey put me right. "I think that's quite a lot to ask," she said. "I don't agree with the view that pets don't need a lot of training and a lot of work; that you can somehow leave them alone and they'll automatically grow into well-behaved animals. It's a real achievement to have a well-behaved dog. It's something people should be proud of having."

She is right, of course. My proudest moments have been when my four have been spontaneously applauded in public for their good behaviour, or people have stopped me in the street to tell me what a credit they are to me. There's nothing to beat that feeling!

111

Prudence and Samson "Boxing"

Six of the Best ... Golden Rules

Golden Rule Number One: Happiness

Training can, and should, be fun. You must devote time to your Golden puppy so that he knows you are wonderful. Does your Golden look at you and yawn? Does he look at you and head off in the opposite direction? Does he look at you and start looking worried? Then some corrective action needs to be taken – with yourself, not the dog. Start smiling a bit more; be a bit more enthusiastic and a little less harsh; start laughing more often; don't be so earnest. Give lots of praise and keep wonderful things for him to eat in your pocket.

Let him know that you are where the action is, that you have the food, and that you are there to help him along life's rough road with lots of praise and lots of love.

Golden Rule Number Two: Play

"Play is so important," Erica says. "If people can play the right games with their dog, understand the rules of the game, and be in control of the game, then they are far less likely to have a problem dog later on."

Well-controlled, constructive play is the bedrock of any good human/canine relationship. He needs lots of toys to play with, and he needs you there to show him how exciting life can be. If you are able-bodied, then get down there on the floor with him and use the play time to teach him right from wrong.

If you are not able bodied, then there are many equally effective ways to establish the bond. Throw the ball for him and reward him when he returns. Express delight by clapping and touching. If you aren't able to rush from room to room playing hide and seek as I do, then you could work gradually towards teaching him to fetch items for you – and rewarding him lavishly when he returns.

Erica warns against games that are too 'rough and tumble', as this can lead to problems of unwanted aggression. "If a dog learns that he can grab hold of a toy and pull and growl and snarl in a game, then he's not that far away from doing it for real," she says.

Instead, you need to devise games that will be fun and will develop your Golden's intelligence. Fetch the ball, sit, come, lie down, catch, and such like, should all be lighthearted and well rewarded. Stop or change the game *before* the puppy becomes bored.

Correction should always be positive, so if he does something of which you approve, tell him so – effusively. If he does something of which you disapprove, then just don't encourage the behaviour. Remember, this is the positive school of dog training, so there is to be no smacking, whacking, jerking or shouting. Instead, calmly stop the game and walk away taking the toy with you. Alternatively, divert his attention onto a more constructive pastime.

Golden Rule Number Three: Be Positive

There's a saying amongst the dog trainers within the British Police Force: 'A dog's temperament travels down the lead'. By this they mean that a dog's behaviour is often reflective of the handler. There are three ways to ask your Golden to do something for you:

1. Get uptight and cross.

2. The Rhett Butler method: "I don't give a damn."

3. Say it, mean it, reward it (be positive).

112

Jet - Aureo Jetoca Jet CDX.SH.WCX

Method one – the angry way – teaches your dog that you are horrible, and you think your dog is horrible too. Little Goldie will either clear off out of the way, develop a nervous twitch whenever you are around, or respond with an equal measure of anger. You won't enjoy it; he won't enjoy it.

Method two – the Rhett Butler method – teaches your dog that he can do it if he likes, and that you can't be bothered if he does or not. If he accidentally follows your command, he won't get any reward – so why should he put himself out?

Method three – the positive way – helps your Golden to understand exactly what is expected of him. In the early days, while you are both learning, you should ask him to do something only when you are reasonably sure he will obey. This is very important: don't ask him to do anything unless you believe he is going to respond. To do this, you need to know you have his attention.

Hey! I said you must have his attention!

You must ask him once, and expect the correct response. If he doesn't respond, then take immediate action to ensure he does (see the individual commands, later, to find out how). Then thank him for his pains with lots of praise and the occasional edible reward. This way, your Golden learns that there is nothing more pleasurable than to work with you as part of a team.

113

Could you get off my chest please? Please?

Golden Rule Number Four: Communicate

If your happy, loving, Golden doesn't do something when you ask him to do it, then he probably doesn't understand what you want.

Training should be based upon talking to your friend, and on a careful consideration of the way his mind works. Because Goldens are so intelligent, they often understand what you are saying when you talk to them. But they are also capable of misunderstanding.

Assuming that you have reached the stage where your Golden wants nothing more than to please you, you need to communicate exactly what it is you want. For example, if you want him to fetch the lead, show him what the lead is, where it is, and name it: 'lead'. If you want to teach him to sit, tell him what he is doing when he is sitting.

Keep commands simple. For example, don't say: "Sit, good boy, sit down, that's it sit. Sit down." How many times do you want him to sit? Do you want him to sit, or do you want him to go into the down position? Why is he being called a good boy, if he hasn't done as you ask? (If you're confused, think how your Golden must feel!)

If you want him to sit once, on the first command, say it once – but only if you know you have his attention. You can't communicate if he isn't listening.

I have found that by clapping my hands during play, this has a positive effect when I want my Goldens to do something for me: when I want their attention I clap my hands. They prick their ears up and look my way in anticipation. Eye contact works wonders, too.

Golden Rule Number Five: your Golden's name is not a swear word

It is only natural to call someone's name when you want him to come to you. However, if you use his name negatively, you are teaching him to run off in the opposite direction (as I know from experience). I know how I'd react if someone shouted: "Catherine, come here you blasted **!!@@*!" Dogs don't like verbal abuse any more than humans do.

Only use your Golden's name when it is associated with good things. He will then *want* to come to you when you call.

If your Golden is digging up the flower beds and you wish to stop him immediately, make a sound that is associated with fun: a sound you use in play, such as hand clapping. Alternatively, go to the spot, point to the plants, and say "No." Then divert the animal's attention to a more constructive pastime. I'm not claiming this method is easy – you have to think about it!

Golden Rule Number Six: Quality time

Not only is it wrong to bring a Golden into your home and then consign him to a life of endless boredom, it is also very short-sighted. If you can't give him fun things to do, he will devise his own games – games that you might not want him to play.

It's only fair to the dog – both puppy and adult – that you should devote some time to him. My four sit quietly by my desk while I work – but when the evening comes, it's over to them. Who wants a miserable dog in the house, one who is expected to sit in the corner all the time? What's the point?

Also on the subject of quality time, make sure that your training sessions do not go on for too long and consequently develop into boring, tedious time. Keep lessons short – a few minutes, little and often

"One must wonder how many diseases are brought on as a result of man's influence on aninmals - whether by translocation, breeding hereditary faults, misuse, wrong diets, and so on. Whether or not this is the case, we have a fundamental obligation to do our best for them when they succumb because we have placed them in a position of total dependance on us."

Christopher Day

114

Sophie, Pru and Samson love to play together

Basic Commands

Toilet training

One thing is for sure: your puppy *will* mess in the house. You have to expect it, it's part of being a puppy.

Anticipation is therefore the Golden Rule. When a puppy is very young, take him out ten or fifteen times a day. At this stage you must think for the puppy, and take him straight out as soon as you see him circling, sniffing the ground or looking agitated. He should also go out after meals and when he wakes up.

It's no good shoving him out in the garden on a cold December night and expecting him to do the right thing. You need to go out with him and keep him company. When he does it, praise him lavishly. This teaches him that it is right to do it in the garden.

If you have failed to anticipate in the house, but catch him in the act, shout "NO!" loudly. This should startle him out of his present course of action, and you can swiftly move him outside where you can praise him for his good behaviour. Do take care, though, that you don't overdo this – the puppy shouldn't just think of you as that awful person who shouts and frightens him. He needs lots of praise to compensate.

There is also no point in reprimanding your Golden if you are too late to catch him in the act. Even if he did it a second ago, he won't be able to understand why you are telling him off later. He has to be caught before or while he does it, or you must simply clear up the mess and resolve to be more alert next time. Punishment is destructive when toilet training.

115

No!

'No' is the one negative we allow into the positive school of Golden training. But it must be said in a positive way. "No you may not do that, but you can do this..."

If your puppy is eating your best shoes, then it's your own fault – you shouldn't leave them lying around!

If he is biting your hand, you need to tell him No, and give him something else to bite (like an old towel or a chewy bone). If he is wriggling and squirming while you try to brush him, then calm the situation down by stroking and try to make the event a pleasant one. If absolutely necessary, stop and wait until he is less lively. (Stop on a good note.)

In short, if you are stopping your puppy from doing something unacceptable, you should always find something positive for the puppy to do instead. Never, ever, smack or hit. It's unnecessary.

Sit

Sit is the primary control command, the most important command. When your Golden obeys this command, you are in control, and you, your children and your Golden are safe. One day, for example, he may decide to run after sheep. If you've got the sit routine right, then you can avert a disaster.

You can teach your puppy to sit without even touching him!

Conventional wisdom suggests that you put your hand on his chest and another on his bottom and push him into the sit position. Ours is a different method.

Erica: "For a dog to sit, his head has to go up and backwards. First, use a titbit to get the attention of your puppy. Then move your hand with the food up and backwards – not so high that the dog jumps up, but just between his ears." It's brilliant, most pups will sit when you do this.

When he sits, let him know what he is doing. Use the word: 'sit' – with a nice crisp pronunciation – but say it once only. Do not attempt this exercise unless you have his attention and you are consequently reasonably sure he will obey.

After a while, you won't need to use the titbit all the time. The occasional surprise focuses the mind beautifully.

Stay

Stay is an extension of sit. Put your dog into the sit position using the above method. Do not give the titbit immediately, but wait a few seconds and say 'stay'. If the puppy does indeed stay, give him the titbit and lots of praise. Gradually increase the time between sitting and rewarding.

He needs to know when he is allowed to move, so there should be a release word. OK, off, let's go – any of these will do so long as you are consistent. The reward, however, should be for staying, not for moving.

Prolonged stay

Conventional training can confuse a dog! With traditional methods, the dog is taught to sit and stay and he is berated for moving. Then the owner walks to the other end of the room and calls him – telling him to do exactly the thing she has already told him off for.

In the positive school of dog training, the stay and the recall are taught totally separately. Stay means don't move from there and I will praise you and reward you for staying.

Tell your puppy to sit and stay, as with the previous exercise. Ask a friend to stay with your puppy so that he or she can hold him while you go out of the room. Go back in immediately and reward him for staying.

Once you have got to the stage where the puppy is happy to stay because he knows you are coming back (the pleasure of your company is the reward), extend the time you are away. With much practice, you will be able to get him to stay without the aid of your friend.

The recall

A successful recall is greatly associated with the fact that your Golden loves you and he actually wants to be with you. It means that wherever you are, he will leave that wonderful smell, the other dogs he is playing with, or the person he wants to say hello to, and come to your side.

To begin with, work on your relationship so that he is always happy to come when he hears you call his name. In addition to verbal rewards (gooooooooood boy!), give food rewards. Most people stroke and caress their Goldens as a matter of course (while watching TV for example), so a piece of cheese, liver cooked in garlic, or yeast tablets add an extra incentive. Obviously, you need to be sure that you are not turning little Goldie into Porky Pig – so only small pieces of cheese. Yeast tablets are non-fattening.

I use the word 'here' when calling my four, always prefixed with the particular dog's name. However, Erica points out that 'here' is very similar to the word 'heel' and could cause confusion. 'Come' would probably be better. Use the words that are most natural to you, but bear in mind that they should be distinct from other control words.

When we're out on a walk and need all four to come, we call 'this way', and walk in the opposite direction. A dog is more likely to follow you if you are walking away from him than if you are walking towards him. Similarly, if you want your dog to come to you as a matter of urgency, attract his attention and run off in the opposite direction. He is extremely likely to follow.

Also, when I walk past any of my four on a walk, I give a sharp whistle which has taught them that I'm not hanging around waiting for them, that if they want to be with me, they have to come.

Note: When I 'round up' stray dogs in the village, my neighbours always ask me, with bemusement, how I manage to get the dog to come to me. The answer is in the question: they come to me, I don't chase after them. You will never catch a dog by following it. The trick is to persuade it to follow you.

Make warm and interesting sounds; smile. Crouch down so that you and the dog are at the same level. Wait patiently for the dog to approach you – never lunge at it – and stroke him affectionately and sensitively when he comes. Allow the dog to move away again so that he knows you are not just there to trap him (it helps the next time he runs away from home). Tell him how beautiful he is: become friends. Praise him when you put his lead on, and obtain his co-operation when you lead him home; don't drag him.

Lie down

Following the same principle as the 'sit' command, teach your dog to lie down by directing his nose downwards and forwards. Hold a delectable morsel in your hand and move it down and away from your Golden's nose, towards the floor. Once he is lying down, say 'down', and give praise as well as the titbit.

It also helps to tell your friend what he is doing when he is doing it. When he lies down as a matter of course, tell him what he is doing. Say, 'down', and praise.

Note: If you use the word 'down' to stop your puppy from jumping up or to get him off the furniture, then find another word to tell him to lie down.

(Chappie proves to me that negative training can have a long-term effect. Tell him to lie down and his happy smiling face turns into one of utter rejection and despondency. I suspect, but cannot know, that it was used as a punishment in his first home.)

Socialisation

Socialisation is an important part of your Golden's development. You can imagine how frightening the world can be to a young puppy. There are all sorts of smells, sounds, textures, and sights to get used to. Is that loud noise the end of the world, or is it a dustbin lid rattling? Has the sky fallen on my head, or was it an acorn?

Before you take your Golden out for his first walk, you need to take the time to familiarise him with the sights and sounds he will encounter. He should also be taught to walk on a lead long before his inoculations are complete.

Whilst John was taking the older three out for their morning constitutional, I used a small collar and lead to play with Samson in the house. We would dash around the house, me following him – because he's got a mind of his own – and I'd make sure that the lead didn't pull him in any way.

If your Golden is more willing to follow your lead, then encourage him forward with lots of happy words. Do not pull him about by the neck, but obtain his co-operation.

Once Samson was used to the lead, we began to venture outside and walked up the drive together. To begin with, Samson thought it was great fun to skit all over the place, but with gentle coaxing, he soon realised that we were *going somewhere*. Again, don't use the lead to pull your little friend along, but go down on your haunches and call him to you in warm and friendly tones.

Then sit and watch the cars go by, making sure, of course, that he can't run out into the road. Sit down and caress him whenever a car or a lorry hurtles past, and this will prove to be useful when he is on his first real walk.

Make an effort to get your Golden used to all sorts of environments and noises while he is young. You can, for example, imagine how frightening it could be for a year-old Golden to be suddenly introduced to a city centre.

Take time, also, to introduce him to other dogs once vaccinations are complete. Invite your friends round with their trustworthy canines, and supervise the interaction. Make sure the puppy isn't taking liberties, because adult dogs are very tolerant of puppies. The adult may be harmed by the puppy's sharp little teeth or, alternatively, once he is around six months old it will come as a surprise to him to discover that he is no longer tolerated.

Be cautious with strange dogs in the park. Stay close to your puppy so that you can supervise any interaction. Conversely, don't send out signals that will teach him to be frightened of strange dogs. If you move over to the other side of the pavement when you see a dog coming, for example, you are only teaching him that there is something to fear.

Walking to heel

Once again, we are going to turn conventional training methods on their head. In the positive school of dog training, there is to be no yanking your Golden about by the neck. This means that choke chains are definitely out. If you have trouble accepting this, put a choke chain around your bare arm and ask someone with a sense of humour to give it a good jerk!

Choke chains are responsible for a great deal of discomfort, bruising, and spinal injury. They are also unnecessary. Training your Golden should be a wonderful experience for you both. It should be really good fun, something that everyone enjoys.

Bearing in mind that reward is your Golden's primary motivation, ask yourself why a dog might pull on the lead...

Could it be that he is anxious to get somewhere?

If you continue moving, you are rewarding his efforts to pull you forward – because the reward is literally forward movement. If you stop, he is no longer being rewarded for pulling.

If your Golden pulls on the lead, stop. Bring him to you (don't yank, guide him gently) and praise him. Then move off. Stop again if he pulls and bring him to you. If he is walking along without pulling, and the lead is slack, tell him what a good boy he is. Keep on doing this until he gets the message. It may take some time, but it is kind and effective.

By talking to your friend as you walk along, he will begin to understand where you want to go, and he will happily go with you. I say 'this way' which is a warning for my four to be on the alert and change direction in line with my steps. Guide Dogs for the Blind are taught to respond to the words 'left' and 'right'.

For people who are physically infirm or families with children, the headcollar is to be highly recommended. It's also ideal for the boisterous Golden with an intense zest for life: the character who is terribly eager to get there.

The headcollar works on the same principle as the headcollar used for horses. Rather than relying upon control by the neck, the headcollar leads a dog by the head. It miraculously stops any pulling; it is safe; and it is comfortable for the dog. (Like a normal collar, it will take a little while for your dog to get used to it – but persevere because it works wonders.)

If you use the conventional collar, don't go for a little thin one. For the adult Golden it should be at least one inch in width to minimise any risk of damage to his neck.

Home alone

At some stage you will need to leave your Golden Retriever home alone. To avoid anxiety attacks on the part of the dog, teach him that you are not going for ever, and that he will be engulfed in love and affection when you return.

Choose times when your puppy has been active and is tired and ready for a sleep, after a good walk or a game, for example. Go out of the room and close the door behind you, and return within a few moments. Do not enter the room if he starts to scream or react against your departure, because this is rewarding him for making a fuss.

Instead, if he is howling, open the door without going in. Do not reward him with any attention when he comes to you. Next time (not immediately), go out for only a few seconds, and return *before* he has time to howl. Give him lots of praise and affection if he is awake and has noticed your absence.

Gradually extend the time you leave the door closed and, each time, go back and give love.

Extend the exercise by popping into the garden without him – again, while he is asleep. If he notices your absence without fussing, give him lots of praise when you return. When you need to go shopping, do so when he is tired. Praise him when you return – whatever the scene that greets you upon your arrival.

116

Thea made it quite clear that Ed. and Marallyn had be away too long. Who say's a dog can't talk?!

If you go out for a long period of time and are greeted with havoc and mayhem and your personal possessions in shreds, this is a sign that he was either bored, or frantically anxious. Do not punish.

If anxiety is the cause, work harder to put him at ease and show that your return – the reward – is a joyous event. (Try a sneak look through the window after you leave – you will be able to see whether he is in distress, or whether he lies down calmly for a sleep.) If he has obviously been bored, leave toys and safe bones as an outlet for his natural playfulness.

In the meantime, it may help to simulate the living conditions he is used to while you *are* around. Leave a radio playing or the television on, leave as many doors open inside the house as you dare, and remove any items you do not wish him to chew.

Mary's Little Lamb

If your Golden Retriever follows you about like a little lamb, this is wonderful because you have established the loving bond that makes him want to please you. However, in excess, this can cause problems if you need to be away.

If your darling is overly dependent upon you, withdraw a little of your affection. Don't sit and fuss him all the time, don't play with him all the time. In short, don't give him all your attention. Teach him that it is not the end of the world if you are not there, because you were being really boring anyway.

Also, take time to introduce him to other people so that he knows you are not the only nice person in the world.

Samson, Prudence and me enjoying the flowers

117

The Golden Oldie

What do you do if you acquire an older dog who has developed all the bad habits? What do you do if *you* have allowed your dog to develop bad habits? How can you teach an old dog new tricks?

Having obtained Chappie as a rescue dog at 18 months of age, and having inherited a dog with a strong independent streak anyway, I know that the task is not so easy. Poor old Chappie, it seemed, had been beaten into submission – and being our first Golden, he also suffered in our hands: he was at the rough end of all our mistakes.

(Ann Bonner's Molly, on the other hand, came to the family when she was seven, and she obeyed Ann from the start – so don't let this put you off rescue dogs.)

Encouragement, patience, love and understanding are needed in great measure where the older dog is concerned. You need to be firm, but not cruel. And you need to try and see things from his point of view.

An older dog who has been pushed and pulled about in order to make him sit is going to resist all the more when you try to teach him. The methods outlined previously may not work. You may have to teach him to sit with his back to a wall so that he can't wriggle away or walk backwards to take the titbit.

It may take time for you to gain his trust and his affection. He may not come to you when you call him, because he has to unlearn the sad lesson that says he will be beaten or verbally abused when he comes. It will be necessary to put him in environments where it is impossible for him to run away when you call, and train gradually over time.

You will need to think that little bit harder, and have extra patience. You will have to surprise him – show him that he now gets praise where once he got anger.

You need to out-think him, try to discover why he is doing what he is doing – what are the rewards he seeks, what is he seeking to avoid, what are the circumstances in which unwanted behaviour seems to occur?

The dog who is destructive: how can you divert his attention onto more positive pastimes? Ask yourself why he is being destructive. Is he bored? Is he anxious? Does he have excess energy to work off? Remember, he is *not* being deliberately naughty just to annoy you. There's a reason behind the behaviour, and the behaviour can be modified.

119

Many people say that dogs obey you to receive rewards, so you have to be careful and consider what it is you are rewarding. The following example, however, illustrates that you must divest yourselves of all preconceptions where the older dog is concerned:

When we first took Chappie out for walks, he would sit down and refuse to budge if we walked past the entrance to the field. I was surprised to discover that he then cringed, expecting me to hit him. Instead, I crouched down and caressed him. This time it was Chappie's turn to be surprised. Some might think that Chappie now sits down and refuses to budge when he wants a cuddle . . . no. He's happy to walk *with* me when I talk to him in warm and friendly tones; he is reassured when my eyes smile into his. We're friends, and he's happy to come along.

118

Training classes

Puppies, adult dogs, and human beings benefit from training classes. They enable you to socialise your dog in a positive way and, if you have problems, there are plenty of people there to offer advice and guidance. They can also be great fun.

It is important to ensure that the class you join is suited to the Golden personality – if he isn't enjoying it, then think carefully about attending. On the whole Goldens are sensitive, gentle dogs, and they do not respond well to the "do as I tell you or I'll thump you" training style.

We took Chappie and Sophie along to a special class for Golden Retrievers which was run by a well-respected German Shepherd trainer, and we nearly died when he picked Sophie as a demonstration model and yanked her about the room. She was extremely frightened to say the least. Neither were we encouraged to see Goldens cringing away from the trainer whenever he walked near them. Goldens (and most other breeds for that matter) just don't need forceful dictatorial handling and brute force.

The trouble is, most people have been taught that it is acceptable to manhandle dogs in order to train them. They aren't unkind or nasty people, they even love dogs. They are teaching what they have been taught.

If you like, and succeed, with the behavioural style, don't discount your local training school. Go along and take a look – you may well find that it is a wonderful place. You may even become a positive influence.

Finally, Erica Peachey urges that you don't try this method and then give up. It will take patience, intelligence, and time – but it works long-term.

Behavioural Problems and their Solutions

A few of the most common behavioural problems are outlined below. This is not an exhaustive list because behavioural problems can and do merit a book in their own right.

The Boisterous Golden

If you are one of the fortunate people who has a boisterous Golden, then you have the happiest, jolliest, merriest, funniest source of companionship you could ever hope to meet. This is one friend who will never be boring. (Just as I was writing this I heard a little bark from Samson and some furious scratching which meant he was up to no good. Upon investigation, Samson had been playing 'let's unravel the toilet roll and shred it all over the floor'. He's been watching too many television commercials!)

Which illustrates, rather nicely, that there is a time and a place for everything.

The boisterous dog is telling you that he wants to play. Having invited him in, as part of your life, you can't just tell him he can't play, ever. There must be a time for playing, and a time for quiet. He needs to know that this is so.

The playful puppy shouldn't be forced to go away and amuse himself, because he will amuse himself like our Samson did, chewing up your cherished possessions, or toilet roll. Instead, give him half an hour of your time, play with him, wear him out – and suddenly the boisterous puppy becomes a happy, steady puppy. Increase the length of his walks, also, to use up that excess energy.

It will take a little while for your puppy to get into the routine, so in the meantime, enjoy his puppyhood if you can and spend time playing with him as he grows.

There must also be a special time in the day, every day, when your adult Golden knows he is allowed to play. During this time he must be allowed to be himself, to charge around and be a lunatic under your control. This might be walking, playing, fussing, or all of these.

It then comes naturally that during the rest of the time, the quiet time, your Golden is happy to lie down and be quiet. (In fact if I'm late starting work in the morning, Samson has been known to grab my arm and walk me to my desk so that he can get some sleep.)

If your Golden is so boisterous that he's a plain nuisance, what should you do? Some people keep the nuisance locked up in the kitchen or outside in a run. Then when he comes indoors, they work with all their might to stop him from clawing at guests and ripping their clothes to shreds. Pretty soon, he's not invited in at all.

But of course he's going to be boisterous if you keep him locked away for hours on end and starved of company!

It must be said that it is unfair to leave a Golden Retriever at home all day while you go out to work. It's downright cruel to leave him all day and then refuse to play with him in the evening. My advice, if you have to leave him all day, is to consider getting another dog to keep him company. You need to be sure, though, that they get on well together, and you should realise that if you have two dogs, then they each need quality time from you.

If you can't devote time to him in the evening, then think seriously about the quality of life your Golden enjoys – is it fair to keep him?

Our Goldens have the run of the house. They are never, ever, locked away when friends arrive; they are never left at home alone for more than four hours, and even this happens very rarely. When friends arrive, they take a few moments to say hello, and then they fall asleep. This is their home too and, as a result of our 'liberal' attitude, visitors usually remark upon how well behaved they are.

If any of them overstep the mark and become too boisterous, I stop them by telling them 'No' very quietly, and very lovingly. Once they have stopped, I bring them to me and stroke them while we talk, and they soon settle down. Believe me, it's worth persevering and giving *more* time and *more* attention – the whole thing will cease to be an issue if you do.

The Barking Golden

Humans sing, shout and chatter; dogs bark. You can't go round and complain about the dawn chorus, either. Barking is part of being a dog. There is no way you can stop a dog barking, any more than you can stop birds singing. In any case, many of us are grateful to our friends when they bark to warn away would-be intruders.

However . . . we don't all have neighbours who appreciate our burglar alarms when they carry on barking for what is deemed to be an unacceptable length of time. The solution, then, is to thank the dog for raising the alarm, and reward him when he stops.

Having put up with Samson barking excessively for 20 months (not continuously , I hasten to add), I came upon an article written by David Appleby in 'Dogs Today' magazine. His advice was: when the dog barks, say "speak" and praise the dog. Then ask him to stop and praise him for stopping. Pretty soon, you can have your dog barking on command, and stopping on command. It took us less than a week to cure Samson of his noisy behaviour! Brilliant, and positive!

Chewing

Here's another one: all puppies chew. It's up to us as owners to be aware of this fact and teach them what is right to chew and what is not.

When you are with your puppy, make sure he is chewing on something acceptable. In very young puppies it should be something fairly soft (a hand towel, for example). As he grows older, smoked bones and toys can be used. Make sure the toys are reasonably Goldie-proof. Many of the toys you can buy in pet shops are unsuitable for Golden Retrievers – they are too flimsy and your Golden will just wreck them. They might also harm him. Please note, Golden Retrievers adore socks. Some Goldens may even swallow them whole which could lead to an intestinal blockage. If your dog is a sock swallower, then this game should cease.

In any event, you should keep a close eye on your young friend to see he is safe with his toys.

Kong toys come highly recommended. They are made of natural rubber and formed into a beehive-type shape. They are flexible, so they give when the dog chews, and they bounce at different angles to give unpredictable amusement.

Diversion is the primary training method for the chewing pup: tell him No when he chews something you don't want him to chew, and replace it with something he may chew.

If you are not there to tell him what he may not chew, it is quite understandable that he may get it wrong. Remove all items you wish to safeguard.

It's also worth remembering to put any dangerous objects out of reach. Take a look around your house and make sure he's not going to kill himself by chewing on razor blades, plastic bags, shoe buckles, and so on. Antifreeze is poisonous; drawing pins and needles get left lying around; and some balls are so small that the dog can choke on them (golf balls, for example).

Finally, puppies and older dogs may chew their way into the carpet, concrete floor, central heating system, telephone wires and more while you are away. This could be caused by anxiety or boredom. If caused by anxiety, punishment will simply accentuate the problem. If caused by boredom, take another look at the 'Home alone' and 'Boisterous' sections.

Jumping up

All dogs jump up to express their pleasure at meeting people. I rather like it when my Goldens jump up at me, and they like it so much that we always get joyous welcomes – even when the dogs have been out with us as well! As soon as we walk through the front door it's 'hello mummy, I know I saw you two seconds ago, but I'm jumping up anyway; isn't life wonderful'.

I do understand that visitors to the house might not appreciate the compliment, and their silk suits may not withstand the attention. Similarly, if you have elderly people or young children in the house, a great big lumbering Golden could cause serious damage when he jumps up.

Anticipation is the key to success. Stop him before he jumps by giving the sit command and praising him for sitting. If you are too late, quickly guide his body down and tell him to sit. Teach children to put their hand on the dog's head and say "Down" in a deep, firm voice. Encourage children not to run away or turn their back as this accentuates the problem.

A dog is only jumping because he has learned that he gets attention for it. Give him attention for staying down instead.

Goldens and Children

If you have children, and are thinking of getting a Golden, then think carefully. It is true that most Goldens get on famously with youngsters, but it is vitally important that you realise you will have the equivalent of another child in the house.

A Golden Retriever is not the sort of dog you can expect to mind his own business and speak when spoken to. You will need to put the time in to train him (can you spare it?) and he will need to be fully involved as part of the family. It's only just that he receives his fair share of time and attention. It's also sound common sense, too. For without your time and attention, that intelligent Golden Retriever will quite possibly become a juvenile delinquent.

Graham Hall, owner of Show Champion Stirchley Saxon, expresses the point beautifully: "We had to re-home a dog recently. There's nothing at all wrong with the dog. He was only ten months old and he was playing and got too rough. He's a bit boisterous; he's a big lad, about 70lbs in weight now, but I don't think they allowed him the freedom he needed.

"His owners had two children and he wasn't allowed to pick up the children's toys. They tried to segregate the dog and the children, and the dog didn't understand. If he's got a toy, and they've got a toy, then he's part of the pack and they should all live together and play with each other.

"He's living with a couple who love hill walking now, and he has settled in beautifully. The only thing he's done wrong so far is to re-arrange some cushions."

It is true that most Goldens are usually wonderful companions for children. But there are also potential problems which need to be addressed before they happen:

* A fully grown Golden Retriever is a force to be reckoned with when he's having fun, and the over-exuberant Golden could knock a child flying without meaning to.

* Don't be surprised when a Golden Retriever does what he's bred for and retrieves Johnnie's toys. I personally think that one or two chewed items act as a marvellous incentive to tidyness.

* Puppies have sharp teeth and they don't understand that they are not supposed to bite.

* Children aren't always angels, either. If left unsupervised they may well do dreadful things like climb on his back, pull him about by the neck, yank his tail, poke pencils in his ear, kick him, hit him . . . don't be surprised if the Golden defends himself in these circumstances and bites back.

It is important, therefore, to teach your children how to play, and to teach your Golden how to respond. The first rule is to teach the children that they need to respect the dog's space. If he's lying down in his bed, it is unfair to allow them to bother him. Everyone needs to be quiet from time to time.

Never, ever, leave children alone with Goldens, or vice versa unless you are sure the children understand how to behave in the company of a dog, and that you can trust your Golden to be gentle. Spend time watching how they play together beforehand. Spell out the rules.

Rough and tumble games should be discouraged because a puppy could begin to think of the child as a litter mate – and we all know how rough games can be between two young puppies. The older Golden could get carried away and inadvertently hurt a child or, alternatively, the child could get carried away and inadvertently hurt the dog.

Instead, teach your child how to play positive games with the dog. Fetch, sit and come, are good examples. Be sure, though, that your over-enthusiastic child isn't exacting corporal punishment to achieve his objective.

It's good for the child and for the dog if children are given something positive to do. Perhaps your children could be responsible for feeding (supervised to ensure that your pet has the nutrients he requires). Perhaps they could be in charge of walkies after school, providing the child is capable of controlling the dog. Involve children with the dog's care and they too will learn many valuable lessons about life, communication, kindness, and responsibility.

The product of love and affection – case story

Twelve-year-old Barry Phillips wanted a puppy so desperately that he saved up the earnings from his paper round to buy her. "We went to visit Erica Ward of the Fernavy kennel," said Shirley Phillips, his mother, "and Barry picked out a beautiful little bitch. Erica was very helpful, and gave us a great deal of advice about bringing the puppy up."

Shirley and Barry struck a deal: "I told him that I would toilet train Leasha, but it was his duty to train her on the lead. I think that it is good for a child to cultivate a sense of responsibility early on.

"Barry did a fabulous job, and took on his task with all seriousness, getting up in the early hours of the morning to walk her before he went to school. In fact, he had her so perfectly trained that we rarely needed to use the lead. Leasha was so good that she would walk to heel. She would never cross a road unless we told her she could, and she would never chase cats."

Now an adult, Barry has obviously benefited from his parents' philosophy. Working and living now in Strasbourg, Barry Phillips is training to be a barrister at the European Court of Human Rights. He says, "being able to have a dog at an early age, with the responsibility of training her and looking after her, formed a bond between the two of us. It also taught me to respect the place in this world for animals. Having had to save up and pay for Leasha myself helped me to keep the interest in her, and it also made me very proud of her when she was admired. She gave me a real sense of achievement."

120

Leasha

Unlike the conventional chapter on breeding to be found in most dog books, this chapter discusses the pros and cons of breeding, the whys and wherefores, and the effort you will find yourself expending should you decide to take the plunge. It does not go into the biological chain of events, because there are many good books which can do this in far greater detail, and their authors offer credentials which are far superior to my own.

There are, after all, so many things to consider. You'll want to look at your bitch's physical appearance and temperament and decide whether you wish to replicate them. You'll need to have her hips and eyes examined to make sure they're up to standard. You'll need a considerable amount of time. And you will have to find good homes for any puppies that arrive.

Caution

My American friend, Mike Grubb, has appealed for the discussion on breeding to be expanded. "Ever since President Ford had Liberty, his Golden, in the White House," Mike said, "the breed's popularity in the US has skyrocketed, resulting in Goldens being bred in puppy mills to stock the pet shops, plus every backyard breeder around cranking out as many litters as possible.

"We see litters advertised all the time, selling Goldens for $400 and more. We call and the people don't know what we are talking about when we question them about hip dysplasis, cataracts, SAS, temperament, and so on. Rescue organisations are needed because of this massive overbreeding. It is heartbreaking to think of all the Goldens that are born for the quick buck and end up at the end of a rope, tied up and forgotten in somebody's back yard. My plea to all breeders is make sure you are really contributing something to the breed before you have another litter."

I have found that the very top breeders produce puppies very very rarely. They do so, predominantly, to bring on an up and coming champion for their own kennel. They then choose owners for the remaining puppies with extreme care. Similarly, owners of the very best stud dogs are very 'pickey' about who they allow to mate with their champ.

John Seymour represents an excellent case study of a person who has bred from his one Golden bitch. John was so conscientious, so thorough, and so determined to produce as perfect a litter as possible, that his testimony illustrates the magnitude of painstaking research that is required of the novice, and the sheer hard work involved.

I must also add that a considerable number of John's puppies (or should I say Chloe's puppies) have been snapped up by some of the top breeders in the country. Proof positive that he's done a good job!

John acquired Chloe when she was six months old, and he was told that she was a first class bitch. By the time Chloe reached her first birthday, it was quite clear that she had an exceptional physique, coat and body. John has a spinal injury which prevents him from moving easily, so he didn't feel he could do her justice in the show ring – the way the owner moves is almost as important as the dog's movement. Instead, John chose to do Chloe justice by using her to produce champion progeny.

122

Being a novice, it took John seven months to write to different stud dog owners and ask the questions which he felt were crucial. He asked for a copy of the dog's pedigree; enquired whether their hips and eyes had been tested for hereditary defects; and he asked about their general health and temperament. Eventually, he ended up with the pedigrees of fifteen of the top stud Golden Retrievers in the country. These were photocopied and enlarged so that he could add further information after phoning round and asking more questions. The fifteen were eventually narrowed down to three who were closest to Chloe's own blood line.

John was seeking to produce the very best Golden Retriever puppies, so he pinned the three stud dog pedigrees to the wall and sat looking at them for hours at a time. All were champions, all were in excellent health. All were physically outstanding, had good temperaments, and had passed their hip and eye examinations with flying colours. But who should be 'the one'?

"I went right back through the generations of the pedigrees," said John, "and read about the well known breeders who had produced these marvellous dogs. I soon became pretty knowledgeable about who had bred the top dogs, and started to allocate stars to the charts, highlighting the features and attributes I was looking for, and the stars were growing. But still I couldn't make up my mind."

123

So it was back to the drawing board, and John researched further into the pedigrees and made more telephone calls. Eventually he came into contact with a well-known and highly generous breeder who gave him a mountain of good advice and put him on the right track. "Of course," he exclaimed, "I needed to keep the dark eyes and intelligence in the bloodline. I was able to pinpoint the dog I wanted, and promptly booked the mating."

John and Chloe travelled to the stud dog's home, staying overnight so that Chloe could be mated twice on two consecutive days. Meanwhile, John had spent five months building a whelping box onto the house. He and his sons installed a heater, a television set and a radio – devices which would prove invaluable when the pups were born to help with their socialisation.

The first beautiful puppy appeared at 1.30am and number nine was born at 7.30am. Chloe went into stress for about four hours before she went into labour, so John had plenty of time to watch and prepare. "As soon as she started scratching out a nest," says John, "I knew to get ready. It's a fairly natural experience and, providing you've read all the books, your mind starts working very quickly and you know almost instinctively how to help."

Chloe's pups were all breach birth, so John helped her by cutting their cords, holding each one upside down and rubbing it to get it breathing, and then he gave Chloe the pups for her to clean up. He slept beside Chloe for a week to make absolutely certain that mother and pups remained fit and healthy. "After two or three days," says John, "everything falls into place and they settle down beautifully together."

Now the hard work started, with John telephoning the stud dog owner, top breeders, and the local Golden Retriever Club to ensure the pups were found good homes. The phone started to ring constantly, with people inquiring about Chloe's new puppies. Meanwhile, there was feeding, feeding, and more feeding, and handling and playing with the pups to give them the required level of socialisation.

"Socialisation in their first few weeks is so important," says John. "They need to get used to all sorts of sounds: radio, television, windows closing and pots banging. We took my little granddaughter in and watched her closely so they could get used to children. Puppies can't hear or see for at least 14 days, so when it happens it's like a big explosion to the world. But they've still got that feeling. They can feel the air changing when you open windows, and they can feel your hands as you gently stroke and brush them. It's so important to get them prepared for the outside world."

Working in shifts with his wife Doreen, John then prepared a pedigree certificate for each of the pups. Having gone to a great deal of trouble to find the information himself, he decided to pass the full details on to subsequent breeders, so he put hip and eye scores against every dog and bitch where it was known; kennel club registrations, dates of birth, and merits gained. This alone took him five or six weeks to complete. Names had to be chosen for all the pups, and then it was time to meet and vet all prospective owners.

"You try so hard to ensure that they are going to the right homes," says John. "It can make you ill worrying that you've made the right decision. Finding good homes is the breeder's responsibility, and it's a good idea to plan ahead and give yourself plenty of time to get to know the new owners. You'll feel better in yourself then, before they go."

Finally, John says that anyone who loves the breed must think very carefully before breeding. It is not a decision to be taken lightly. It's hard work and your responsibility doesn't end when the puppy joins its new family: "I try to keep in touch with the new owners, and I'm delighted when I hear the dog's doing well."

When things go wrong

It would be irresponsible of me to include a section on breeding, without mentioning that things can go wrong. Neither would it be honest to suggest that breeding is a huge money spinner. There are much easier ways to make money!

In an ideal world, everything will go well and you will produce a perfect litter of puppies. But this is not an ideal world, and life is rarely straightforward. Think very carefully before you decide to breed from your Golden friend. Your bitch doesn't *need* to have a litter for either her mental or physical wellbeing, and there are thousands of puppies you can go out and choose at your leisure.

Roy and Pat Bartlett have kindly described the nightmare they once encountered when breeding from Tammie. It gives a good indication of what you might expect in the worst case. As a qualified midwife, and having bred a few litters, Pat is a level- headed individual who is unlikely to be daunted by many of the things that can happen during whelping. One of Tammie's litters proved to be the exception.

The day Tammie went into whelp, she somehow seemed to give up on life, Roy and Pat told me. They took her to the vet's and a caesarean section had to be performed. Then while the puppies were being born, their sire died. "Tammie had to be nursed back to health," says Pat. "Just as she was beginning to get better, the puppies came down with the parvo virus."

The litter was only seven weeks old and all the puppies were just getting ready to go to their new homes when the virus struck. "One puppy was ill," says Pat. "She was sick twice, which I wasn't too happy about. I rang my vet and told her there was a funny smell. The vet was excellent and came out immediately. Within 24 hours we had seven puppies at the vet's on drips.

"To see the weight drop off them and the vomit and the blood was horrific. Our vet, Anita White, was excellent: she spent a lot of time with them and saved five out of the seven. When we got them home, the house turned into a special care baby unit. Each puppy had an individual pen and we set about nursing them back to health."

It was a round-the-clock job: Roy and Pat were so frightened that something might go wrong, so Roy slept next to the puppies on a camp bed.

"I lay beside them and somehow managed to wake up if any of them was sick," Roy said. "That went on for three weeks; they needed constant attention. We told all our friends who had animals not to come and visit us, and we were told not to have puppies on the premises for twelve months."

At the time, most puppies died when struck by parvo virus. Roy and Pat's vet bill would have been around £800, but the vet said they had put so much of the effort in to keep them alive, and she had learnt so much by nursing them back to health, that it was, to Roy and Pat's relief, only half that amount.

It is said that the parvo virus takes about two weeks to incubate, which is why you must be quite hard on visitors and relatives. Pat never knew where the virus came from, but she does know that you can never be too careful. "A fortnight before this happened I had been to a show with one of my bitches, and I would never do this again. If you do go somewhere where there are a lot of dogs, you should change all your clothes and wash before you touch the puppies so that you are eliminating as many problems as you can. We now have a special parvo virus foot dip, and all visitors must dip their shoes in this before they see the puppies."

But, thankfully, the story has a happy ending. All the dogs who survived turned out beautifully.

One puppy, Cinders, was hit worst with the virus: she was the last one to come home from the vet's. She started as a lovely healthy puppy and ended up so that you could hold her in one hand. "That puppy never made a sound," says Pat, "she took it all in her stride. And now she's gorgeous. Her new owners love her so much that, to begin with, they wouldn't board her with us in case we tried to keep her!

"Another lady who had one of the dogs knew just how much we had gone through," Pat adds. "She knew how many weeks without sleep we had had to keep them alive, so she said she would let us show her dog just once. We took him to a show, and he came third in his class. It was quite a big class and we were all absolutely over the moon about it. Toby is a beautiful boy, and it's difficult to imagine he nearly didn't survive."

How can you tell whether a person will honour a little puppy with love and attention? How do you know they will provide the best food, spend money on vet bills, and be prepared to walk with it through the pouring rain — simply because they know that exercise to a Golden Retriever is as important as the air we breath? How do you know they won't leave it for hours on end, or neglect it, or mistreat it?

Finding the Perfect Homes for Golden Puppies

Fred Rhodes is a dog obedience trainer from central Washington state. He has trained well over a thousand humans to handle dogs during the past twenty years . . . and he is very clearly a great big softie who loves his canine friends with a passion. At last count, Fred was sharing his life with a Golden Retriever, a Shih Tzu (another of my favourite breeds – they're so solid) and a Labrador.

Fred has also bred Golden Retrievers, and has published many humorous and touching articles relating to his experiences with them. Extracts from 'Muff's first litter' are included here as they demonstrate the lifelong interest Fred takes in the puppies he breeds, and the care he has taken to find them good homes.

"Did Muff know that trouble was brewing when a beautiful lady with coiffured hair, fur jacket, and a lovely dress, arrived with her two young girls to view the pups? Did she sense something was wrong? Muff sat in the whelping box keeping a sharp eye on each pup. At seven weeks she wasn't sure whether she was sad to be losing them or glad to be rid of the pests – but she was still the protective mum. The girls sat down and were immediately drowned in Golden Retriever puppies, to the delight of everyone, human and canine. But Muff seemed ill at ease.

"To me, these seemed like the ideal customers; they were obviously capable of providing the very best home. But I felt uneasy when I saw the look in the lady's eyes as I told her, honestly, about housebreaking, chewing and digging. Did she really expect Muff to have eliminated all those puppy problems at the ripe old age of seven weeks? When I told her to give the puppy a full year to get the puppiness completely out of him, I thought I saw a wince.

"But off went two ecstatic little girls trying to carry half a puppy each, so happy and sweet in their pinafores, long white stockings and patent leather shoes.

"About a year later, my phone rang and I heard an unmistakable West Virginia accent. 'I got yer dog,' the man said, and he explained how he had acquired the young Retriever: Muff had been right.

"The man wanted help in getting the dog registered, so I called the lady's home and a young girl answered. Yes, they had given the dog away to a nice man who promised to take good care of him. The girl explained the dog had soiled the carpet so they had to keep it outside, and it was no fun out there. And the housekeeper didn't like dogs. And it barked.

"I got the forms from the AKC, sent them on, and phoned to check that all was now well. 'Smartest dog in the holler,' I was told by the proud new owner. "Goes with me everwhur, don't even have to tell him to jump in the pickup."

"I told Muff: she forgave my dumb move this one time; but she said be sure to tell the man to tie the pup up close in the pickup so he couldn't get hurt."

Buck's is another tale:

"Big, strong, fearless and totally lovable, that was Buck from the day he was born. He started life as 'Mr Left Rear Hip'; that was where we clipped him to identify him from the other ten. Soon we were calling him 'Pig' because he was first to nurse and last to quit. He didn't need any clipping to mark him; he was clearly the leader of the pack.

"Muff did not have enough nursing places that worked to accommodate eleven pups, so we had to religiously pull pups off and put others in their place. Pig was as stubborn as a bulldozer and as cunning as a streetfighter in getting back on the nipple as soon as we looked the other way. In spite of our supervision, he far outstripped the others in weight gain and development.

"He went to a first-time Golden owner, a couple from Texas with children. Bob was a successful businessman. He seemed only mildly interested in the dog at first, careful to get a quality dog and learn what he needed to know to take proper care of him. Bob entered my beginner's obedience class later, and Buck, as they had named him, confirmed all those things I said about him. He was quite a handful, and I wasn't sure Bob was really enjoying it much. But that all changed later.

"While the dog was young, the family moved back to Texas. They still kept in touch, friends as well as customers. One time while I was in Texas, they invited me to dinner and I saw the mature Buck. What a magnificent animal he was. Muff really blew out all the switches when she produced him. The big, square head was one to put on engraved stationery. But of course it is the temperament and style that makes the breed, and he had that in golden bucketsfull.

"The whole family loved Buck, and he worked full-time to love them back. It was with Bob that he had the special relationship. Buck's life revolved around Bob's time after work. It was obviously important to Bob as well. Their beautiful home was new and expensive, and they had made arrangements in many small ways for Buck to be part of the household without damaging it.

"I felt the true depth of the relationship when I got that inevitable call saying Buck had died. The effect on Bob was devastating. I think it surprised his wife, and perhaps himself. I made my usual pitch about getting another Golden as soon as possible. I firmly believe that is the best therapy. I also know, from first-hand experience, that when you lose one of the great ones, you shouldn't expect to replace them. The thing that makes it bearable is to know that this was a story-book case: Great dog; great family; long, healthy, happy life; wonderful memories."

124

Fred, Bean and Buckshot

Nugget - the circle is closed

"Karen is a very determined young woman. I instantly recognised the name, and even the voice on the telephone sounded familiar, after fourteen years. How in the world did she track me down? (But more on that later.)

"Nugget was dead. The last of Muff's litter to go. The grief in Karen's voice was painful over fourteen years of time and thousands of miles of distance. "She was the most sensitive friend I will ever know. She knew me better than anyone. It was impossible to have a down moment - her ever-wagging tail always brought a smile."

"The surprising thing was that, in spite of the overwhelming grief, she wanted to thank me for giving life to Nugget. How's that for class.

"Nugget was the class of the bitches in the litter. Lean and heavily feathered, she looked great, a real lady. But as all Golden owners know, great looks are just a bonus; the real uniqueness of the breed is their personality. Whelped in 1974, she lived until late 1990, and like all her littermates, was bright and active right up to the end.

"In those fourteen years, I moved from West Virginia to Texas, Colorado, and finally Washington state. Through friends and the AKC she tracked me down. I am honoured that the ties were so strong. The circle of Muff's first litter was now closed. All her babies, like her, are gone.

"As I knew she would, Karen rejected, outright, my recommendation: Get another Golden puppy, soon. Of course it won't be the same as Nugget; don't expect it to be. It will be it's own self; it will have features of personality that are wonderful and funny and cute and remarkable and worthy of all the love and devotion you gave Nugget. Some will be different from Nugget's and some will be, to your astonishment, exactly like Nugget's. Of course you will constantly be comparing her to Nugget, not always to her favour, but that's all right! Do you want to limit your life to only one friend, one neighbour, one mate if you should lose the first one?

"Karen is a very determined young woman. I'll get a call before long about this fantastic puppy and the unbelievable things she does."

When you lose your Golden Friend

The Death of a Loved One

From the very moment you bring a Golden Retriever into your home, you are setting yourself up for a broken heart. For a Golden Retriever lives, at best, for only around fifteen years, and it is likely that you will have to learn to cope with this loss. Very often, people just won't understand your grief. The popular consensus appears to be that it is, after all, *only* an animal.

But your Golden Retriever has two parts: there is the doggie part, and there is the individual part. It could be said that it's not so hard to overcome the 'doggie' loss. You can, after all, go and buy another dog. But the greatest pain comes when you have respected the animal as an individual, a person in his own right with all the mannerisms and ways which mark him out as different to all the other dogs you know.

Few people apart from our family and 'doggie friends' seemed to understand why we were so devastated when Oliver died. Had Oliver been a child or a close relative, there would have been flowers and a funeral, and understanding sympathy from just about everyone. People would have understood if we cancelled meetings or closed the office down for a few days. Instead, it was a case of trying to carry on as usual, and crying in private.

And cry we did – for weeks on end. We couldn't sleep; we barely ate – we just sat there, sobbing and wishing it hadn't happened. There were all sorts of complex thoughts and emotions going on. I was shocked to begin with because Oliver died suddenly, without warning. My head ached so much I thought it might explode, and I had terrible chest pains. I felt sick and confused, and I could hardly see through the tears when I walked Sophie, Chappie and Pru to the places we used to go with Oliver.

We worried for Chappie, Sophie and Prudence, who couldn't cry but who were very quiet and very withdrawn. We made ourselves play with them, and cuddled them, and talked to them. And when we buried Oliver, we comforted them as they said their last goodbyes.

Oh God, we missed him so much. Every cupboard I opened, his nose wasn't there. He wasn't following me around, or looking for the action, or putting his enormous paw on my lap, or stealing my socks, or playing with the others, or making us laugh.

And then I panicked. Had I done something to cause Oliver's death? Had I accidentally knocked him? Was his diet wrong? I searched my memory for tell-tale signs, trying in vain to put the clock back – as if finding the reason might wake us all up from an unreal dream.

Then came the anger. I was angry at God for allowing Oliver to die. I was angry at my neighbours who didn't notice he was gone. And I was angry at all the people who thought he was only a dog. So there I was, walking around sobbing my heart out, and getting cross with people who couldn't really be expected to understand.

I wondered whether other people felt like me when they lost their Golden friend: in pain and isolated, as if this particular brand of grief were judged insignificant. I looked into the whole subject of grief and contacted a few relevant organisations to see if there was any research on the subject. One bereavement helpline told me to 'clear off' because the death of a dog was nothing compared to the death of a human. The counsellor was outraged at my call: how dare I compare my feelings with the feelings of a bereaved parent!

And yet, I reasoned in self-defence, Oliver was my child. I used to look at him and hug him, fit to bursting with the love I felt for him. I put the phone down and sobbed my heart out.

I called a second bereavement helpline, Cruse, and these kind people were much more helpful. They put me on the right course and recommended books for me to read. Soon the reactions of other 'doggie' people began to come through.

When the lovely Blossom died, Michael Grubb wrote: "When your dog dies, society does not really allow you the grieving and memorialising of the animal – an animal more loyal, giving and less treacherous than any human. Isn't that ironic?"

Brenda Lowe of the famous Davern kennels has kept Golden Retrievers for nearly thirty years, and she says that it doesn't get easier when a Golden dies. "We have many graves in the garden now," she said, "and, no, it doesn't get any easier. Usually I can't talk about my dogs for a long time after they've died, and it is harder when you have to make the decision for them.

"I never want my friends to suffer and, once their quality of life has deteriorated to a certain point, they look at you and seem to tell you that they've had enough. You know you are doing the right thing for them, but it doesn't make you feel any better about it.

"I sometimes wonder why I keep dogs – because every time one goes, a little bit of me goes with them."

Michaela Edridge, who has loved Golden Retrievers for many, many years, says: "There's a total guilt feeling if you've had to put a dog to sleep. It doesn't matter how necessary it is, or how ill the dog was, you still feel as if you've arranged their death. It's very hard to get over."

Dorothy Cyster, who works within the caring professions on behalf of humans, and also voluntarily as a counsellor for the marvellous PRO-Dogs bereavement helpline, says: "I believe that the death of a loving, trusting pet can be much worse and far more significant than that of a human being, and we should not be made to feel guilty for feeling grief. I'm sure dogs have souls and deserve to be mourned-for as much as humans."

According to J William Worden, author of the book, 'Grief Counselling and Grief Therapy', the intensity of grief is equal to the intensity of love. It is conceivable, then, that the death of a Golden could represent one of the most traumatic events in a person's life. It's so easy to love a Golden Retriever: their trusting, non-judgmental love is impossible to beat.

Dr Sam Ahmedzai, Chairman of the Society for Companion Animal Studies says, "A pet's death may have as devastating an effect as any human bereavement. The feelings, bodily reactions and social suffering are in many ways the same as if we had lost a close relative."

126

J. LOBBAN

The feelings and sensations you may go through

Studies reveal that bereavement induces physical pain and emotional and mental anguish. You can experience feelings of numbness, sadness, anger, guilt and self-reproach, anxiety, loneliness, fatigue, helplessness, shock and yearning. Physical sensations range from headaches and chest pains to breathlessness and lack of energy.

You may become confused, sense the presence of the deceased, or hallucinate. You might be unable to sleep and lose your appetite, you may dream of your deceased friend, call out for him, and you will almost certainly cry. All of this is normal.

For some, there is eventually a feeling of new-found freedom and relief, particularly where the Golden has been ill and suffering. Dr Stewart suggests that this is a good sign, showing that the bereaved is beginning to able to reinvest their love in another target.

Research also shows that it is necessary to work through to the pain of the grief. It is, according to the experts, healthy and natural – and even necessary – to allow yourself to experience pain when you lose someone you love. Immerse yourself in it.

In typical psycho-speak, Worden calls the final task of mourning: "emotionally relocating the deceased and moving on with life." By this, I believe he means not that you should forget your friend, but that in time you should find a place for him in your heart – a place that leaves room for you to extend your love to others.

And what now?

Many people say that they could not get themselves another Golden, because the pain of losing their friend was almost unbearable, and they couldn't go through that pain again. Several people have spoken to me of the anguish caused by well-meaning friends who have suggested they get another dog. "It's like saying, oh well, never mind that your daughter has died. You can always have another baby'." It is that particular dog, that *person* who is missed.

For us, a seven week old puppy became our rescue package. We decided we had to expose ourselves to the pain of loss again, because that pain was paid for a thousand times over by the joy that preceded it. Sammie will never replace Oliver, but my goodness, he has followed an extremely hard act in the most perfect of ways. Most importantly, Sammie has given us a target for the love we could no longer shower upon Oliver, except in our memories.

You may wonder why we didn't shower that love upon our remaining three Golden friends. Well we did, but all of us – me, John, Chappie, Sophie and Prudence – were missing Oliver so much. When we brought Samson home, the three Goldies went absolutely wild with joy. They needed a new target too.

Typical Grief Patterns

1. Initial Reaction - detachment, calm, normal routine, shock, dazed, unresponsive.

2. Despair - acute grieving, intense anguish, psychological pain.

3. Recovery - Active readjustment, new relationships

Golden Memories

Sunshine

Many of the letters I have received from Golden owners have come from people who have now lost their friends. Without a doubt, Goldens have such an enormous presence that they continue to live on in the hearts and minds of everyone who has been lucky enough to share a life with them.

Mr Collie remembered his dear Lulu's willingness to heed his every word and gesture, and countless memorable moments which were testimony to her amiable disposition. Mrs Phillips wrote about Leasha, saying she was a human being in the wrong skin because she loved people so much. And Mrs Hillier wrote to me and described how, nearly twenty years after his death, she still misses her darling Toki, and tells her grandson stories about her kind and sensitive comedian. One day, Mrs Hillier's grandson Oliver asked:

"Gran, was Toki a *real* dog, or is he a fairy story?"

The answer? Toki was very real, and very very loved. Mrs Hillier has never stopped missing Toki and I don't think I will ever stop missing Oliver – but, oh, I am so thankful that he came into our lives.

So, when you lose your Golden friend, remember that there are thousands of people who know your pain, and whose hearts go out to you in memory of their own dear loved ones.

127

Sunshine

And it's the saddest thing
Under the Sun above
To say goodbye
To the ones you love
But I will not weep, nor make a scene
But say thank you,
Life
For having been

Melanie Safka

Mike Grubb wrote so movingly about the death of Sunshine some years ago, that I have chosen to include his account here.

Sunshine died today. She was only six. The sad part is not that we and her roommates, Gypsy and Blossom, will miss her terribly, but that she was so unfairly robbed of much of her life. Never again will she do the things she loved: chase squirrels off the bird feeder, mice out of the wood pile or frogs across a pond. Never again will she dig up rocks to proudly deposit at our feet or make the long retrieve and return with her wagging tail and smiling eyes. Never again will she howl in protest at being left, or chase snowballs, or roll on that special piece of dirt.

She was always Jackie's dog. From the moment she bounced out of her crate at the Amarillo airport, through her five wonderful years in the woods and ponds of New Hampshire, to the last agonising trip to the veterinarian in New York, they shared the special relationship a dog can have with only one person; only theirs was even more special. Wherever Jackie went, Sunshine was by her side.

When business separated Jackie and I for an extended period, it was Sunshine who slept with her every night, awakening to check with a gentle kiss if Jackie was all right. It was her bark that warned people to stay away and her smile that warmed Jackie's heart. She comforted Jackie by her presence and me by knowing they were together.

Sunshine kept the house running smoothly. When play among the other dogs was too rough, she was "The Enforcer," breaking it up with a warning growl and a well placed nudge. When another dog cried in its sleep, she ran over and awoke it with a vigorous licking of the face.

She inherited both her father Lad's desire for field work and his intelligence. She was capable of understanding conversations and could spell bird backwards and forwards. Her intuitiveness in understanding us and our moods was amazing. Although she could be a ferocious watch dog and a tomboy in the field, she was always a lady who kept herself clean and exemplified dignity; hence her names Red Ruby, Miss Shine and Miss Eleganto.

She left us with wonderful memories. Memories of her first swim at eight weeks, her first retrieve of a duck and her heart-breaking "finish" in the obedience ring as she lifted her nose to nuzzle my hand and a loud "Ahh" always arose from the spectators.

Sunshine left us the memory of her earning her Working Certificate on a beautiful New England spring day and of her being introduced to tracking one day and being certified the next, with her head down, her tail wagging and her small legs churning as she plowed through the field. All these beautiful memories will be with us forever.

We spent her last few days trying to cram the rest of her life into those precious hours. We took her for a swim, threw bumpers and fed her ice cream and peanut butter cookies. We tried to make up for all the times we were "too busy" to play with her. Because she was so uncomfortable from the cancer inside her, we spent most of the time on the porch, where she could smell and watch the birds she used to so frantically pursue. It was a sad, sweet time that went so quickly yet seemed to drag on forever.

Finally, the time came. There was one last hug, one last kiss through a haze of tears and she was gone. Her death left an unfillable void. She was the sweetest, kindest, gentlest, most loyal and unselfish living being we have ever known. We miss her terribly.

Michael Grubb, Connecticut

Oliver said to Samson . . .

Oliver gave the embryonic Samson a big lick, and snuggled close to him to instil confidence into the fragile yet-to-be-born life. The two sat looking down through the clouds and over the villages below: the big green fields and the woods, the children at play, the cows and the sheep grazing quietly on the grass.

"I want you to know," said Oliver, "that you are going to a good home. They'll take care of you there, and love you beyond measure, and they'll understand that you need to be a dog; that you need to play and run in open spaces. They will feed you well, and brush you, and take you to the vet when you don't feel well. They will be proud of you, and take you on holidays, and they will never, ever, hit you.

"I want you to know, Samson, that you have a mission in life. Your mission is to teach humans the joy of living by being happy, and radiating that happiness outwards in great golden rays of sunshine. Show them the pleasure of little things: blue skies and strong fresh winds; early morning mists and evening sunsets. Teach, by example, that life can be wonderful, and friendship can be sweet.

"Make them laugh. Steal their slippers and their Wellington boots; delight in their cuddles. Help Catherine with the washing and the gardening, grab her arm at least once a day – she likes that. Keep John company in the kitchen while he prepares the food, rummage in cupboards, pockets and bags, and be gentle with Chappie – he's such a gentle soul.

"Tell Prudence I miss her, Sophie that I love her, and Chappie how much I cared. Be good, and obedient, and have fun: that's what you're there for, Samson my lad. Tell them we'll meet again. Be Golden."

Oliver said ..

128

.. to Samson

129

The Long Goodnight

As you go
into the long goodnight
take with you
Tears
symbol of loss and devastation
Take with you
Smiles
A smile reflects
remembrance of the past
The wondrous floating years
so grateful for all that
Take with you
Love
nurtured and nourished by your sweet perfection
the purest love — un-asked
and undemanding
Take with you
Pieces of heart and soul
You who enriched my life
gave me new perspectives
coloured my dreams with gold
shared with me
secrets of wild primeval past
and from the depths of your magnetic eyes
hinted a mystic future . . .
Take tears smiles
love — my heart and soul
into your long goodnight

Michaela Edridge

Epilogue

Prudence

Just as this book was being finally prepared for the printers, we discovered that Prudence had contracted leukaemia. She died on Sunday, 20th February 1994.

Somehow, this book has had a great deal to do with dying. In the three years it has taken to write and publish, we have witnessed the loss of Benji, Bo, Wally, Tammie, and Dexter. Lord Northesk, who loved Golden Retrievers, never got to see the book; he passed on in January. Many people have chosen to tell me of the dogs who are no longer with them, except in spirit. And now Prudence, our dear sweet little darling, has gone.

This book is subtitled, 'A Chronicle of Joy'. So why has it formed itself into a book so closely associated with death?

It seems to me that death offers us a choice between two ultimate conclusions, depending upon our own personal beliefs. If you do not believe that the spirit continues after the physical body dies, then death at least represents the end of suffering. If you do believe in a continuity, then the promise of reunion is offered and, according to my researches, there is a place to which our loved ones go, which is lovely and beautiful, and free from pain.

Elisabeth Kubler-Ross, a doctor who has devoted many years to the care of the dying, drew one important conclusion from thousands of near-death experiences related by people around the world: "Many of the patients have spoken of the peace they experienced - beautiful, indescribable peace, no pain, no anxiety. They tell us that all that matters is how much you have loved, how much you have cared; and if you know these things . . . then you cannot possibly be afraid of death."

But what of dogs? There are many human beings who do not credit animals with having personalities, so what hope spirits? I wanted the answer.

Shortly after Oliver died, I took myself to a Spiritualist Church. I had never been before. I walked in off the street, knowing no-one and no-one knowing me. The man at the front was going around the room, telling people about deceased auntie Ethels, and then he came to me.

"I have a little dog here," he said. My heart lurched. "He keeps grabbing at my arm and biting my ear. He won't give in." It was Oliver, arm-grabber and ear-nibbler par excellence. "You have a puppy now," the man said. "I've been asked to tell you that you must allow the puppy to be himself. He's not the same as the one you've lost." It made sense, that message, because John and I had specifically gone out to find a dog with Oliver's personality.

On the afternoon of Pru's death, through a haze of tears, I watched a video so that I could see her in full flight, fit and healthy, and full of life. Then I saw it: Prudence and Oliver boxing and cavorting; their strong fit bodies moving gracefully on the grass; sparks of light flying off them as they made the world a better place by being happy and having fun.

A weight lifted off my shoulders, and the knots in my stomach relinquished their grasp. Oliver and Prudence were together again, together. And waiting to welcome us.

These are the memories I have of Prudence, and in particular, the last four weeks, when we struggled with her to save her life.

I see her loving shining eyes, looking into mine with excitement and anticipation. I see her gay tail held high in the air, her ears pert and ready, her legs prancing and dancing, running to fun. I see her barking at horses, at dogs on the television. I see her in the water, always the one to swim the furthest and try the hardest to get that stick.

I see her defending Chappie against the boisterous Sam, and defending Samson against older strange dogs. I see her protecting me; standing guard on the wall around our house: keeping foreign cats at bay, and gazing contentedly at the moon and the stars. I can still see her breath as it rises into the cold night air.

I see her courage, and her determination. Her struggle to survive. Prudence was never one to be beaten, so she attacked the leukaemia by carrying on. We went on walks together, just the two of us, and she took me to visit all her friends: all the children she had loved in the village where we live. She sought out pussy cats, and was so sad that the two who lived at the top of the drive were no longer there. Their owners had moved on, and Prudence was missing them.

Prudence was very weak during the last few days, but this didn't stop her thinking of me. She took me to people in the street, made me talk to them, then lay down contented because she had taken my mind off things. She marched me to the village community centre and made me go in, even though dogs aren't allowed. And she was happy, because I was talking about her and praising her courage, and Sheila was kind to her, and kind to me.

I can still smell her, and I can feel her. I can hear her little barks and her 'nyom nyom nyom'. Samson is missing her: he keeps running around the house and listening for her sound. He sniffs the earth, then looks at me, and I have to explain that Prudence is gone.

Chappie tried to keep Prudence here, sitting with her and being there while she struggled to survive. When Sophie, Sam and I came home in the car yesterday evening, Chappie came out to greet us, running to the back of the car looking for Pru. And Sophie is trying to cheer us all up. Her heart is breaking, but she's making the effort: becoming her most endearing and instigating fun.

John buried Prudence in her favourite spot, beneath the wall where she liked to sit. But that's just her body. She still lives in our hearts.

Prudence was just a dog. One day, the world will realise what 'just a dog' means. Dogs are healers. They share our sufferings, our trials and tribulations. They make people better just by being there. They don't judge, they just love.

Prudence was my sister, my little sister. Not inferior, just weaker, and needing my protection. She never multiplied a fraction, but she was very, very wise. Prudence gave so much - much more than she ever took.

Some people are unable to see beyond the material or the physical. Underneath the four legs, behind those brown eyes, within that canine form, lies a heart as large as the universe. And no, dogs don't have to help human beings to justify their existence - but they do anyway, in love.

Useful addresses

The Golden Retriever Club (UK)
- available from the
Kennel Club
1 Clarges Street
London
W1Y 8AB

The Golden Retriever Club of America Inc
- available from the
American Kennel Club
51 Madison Avenue
New York
Ny 10010
USA

The Golden Retriever Club of Canada
available from the The Canadian
Kennel Club
100-89 Skyeway Avenue
Etobicoke
Ontario M9W 6R4
Canada

Golden Retriever Clubs in Australia
available from the The Australian
Kennel Council
PO Box 285
Red Hill South
VIC 3937
Australia

The North American Hunting Retriever Association
PO Box 6
Garrisonvill
VA 22463
USA

The Guide Dogs for the Blind Association
Hillfields
Burghfield Common
Reading
RG3 7YG
England

Dogs for the Disabled
Frances Hay House
Banbury Road
Bishops Tachbrook
Leamington Spa
Warwickshire
CV33 9UQ
England

Arthritis Foundation
PO Box 19000
Atlanta
Georgia 30326
USA

Erica Peachey
Pet Behaviour Consultant
5 Grove Road
Hoylake
Wirral
Merseyside
L47 2DS
England

Association of Pet Behaviour Counsellors
257 Royal College Street
London
SW1

Canine Partners for Independence
2 Cyprus Road
Regents Park Road
Finchley
London
N3 3RY

The SOHO Foundation
Stichting SOHO
Postbus 24
5373 ZG Herpen
Netherlands

Canine Companions for Independence
PO Box 446
Santa Rosa
CA 95401
USA

Western Canada's Handi and Hearing Ear Dog Society
10060 #5 Road
Richmond
British Columbia
Canada V7A 4E5

PRO Dogs National Charity - (including PAT Dogs)
Rocky Bank
4 New Road
Ditton
Aylesford
Maidstone
Kent
ME20 6AD
England

Hearing Dogs for the Deaf
Training Centre
London Road
Lewknow
Oxford
OX9 5RY
England

The Seekers Trust

The Close
Addington
West Malling
Kent
ME19 5BL
England

Yankee Golden Retriever Rescue Inc

PO Box 104
N. Reading
MA 01864
USA

Mendip Natural Healing Centre

Great Burrow
Bratton Clovelly
Oakhampton
Devon
EX20 4JJ
England

Green Ark Animal Nutrition

PO Box 1151
Castle Douglas
Galloway
DG8 1RA
Great Britain

Holly Blood Donor Appeal

(blood banks for dogs)
PO Box 95
Dartford
Kent
DA1 1UE

The Cinnamon Trust

(companion animals for the elderly)
Poldarves Farm
Trescowe Common
Germoe
Penzance
Cornwall
TR20 9RX
United Kingdom

The Homeopathic Society

(for list of vets)
2 Powis Place
Great Ormond Street
London
WC1N 3HT
Telephone 071 837 3297

Golden Retriever clubs

There are Golden Retriever clubs in most countries of the world. Contact your national kennel club for the appropriate address (addresses change frequently, so it is inappropriate to list them here).
The Golden Retriever clubs will also provide information about Rescue organisations near you.

Published by

Abbeywood Publishing
PO Box 139
Walgrave
Northamptonshire
England, NN6 9RZ
telephone 0604 781833
facsimile 0604 781919

Professional Credits

Our thanks go to the following professional photographers for the use of their pictures:

Susan Rezy, Danville, IN, USA, pictures 6, 7, 8, 17, 32, 82, 85, 100, 104, 105, 106, 107, 115, 118, 119

R Willbie, Animal Photography Partnership, London, picture 101

Roger White, Chard, England, picture 26

John Roan Photography, Northampton, England, picture 98

Philip Tull, Hungerford, England, picture 33

K Young, England, picture 57

Christopher Bradbury, Leamington Spa, England, picture 46

Albert Rigby, Princes Risborough, England, picture 68

Pedigree Petfoods, picture 67

The Birmingham Post & Mail, England, picture 59

Val Connolloy Photography, Frodsham, Cheshire, England, pictures 56, 80

Sally Anne Thompson, Animal Photography Partnership, Painswick, England, pictures 54, 69

Julianne Houseman Caruthers, Mt. Vernon, USA, picture 112

Illustrations by Janet Lobban, Gwestfa, Carmel, Llanelli, Dyfed SA14 7TN (to commission a work, please send a good sharp photograph of your Golden Retriever)

Our special thanks go to Charles Ward, Northamptonshire, England, for the front cover photograph of Tigger (Clanmaxwell Tigger Too) owned by Mrs Rosemary Arnold of Bozeat, England (thanks Rose);

to Susan Rezy for the full page photographs on pages 17, 81, 101, and 135;

to Val Connolly for the full page photographs on pages 91, 119, and 155;

and to Roy Bartlett for the full page photograph on page 163.

Man, animals, and plants are living expressions of the Grace of the Creator. Man can have a common language with the animals, consisting of the purest thoughts and blessings we bestow upon them. We can talk to animals "mind to mind", and through the silent, universal language of the heart. Love for animals is nourished from the depths of our heart, by the deepest longing of our soul to respond with God's unconditional love (agape) to our fellow earthly creatures.

Joanne Stefanatos D.V.M.
extracted from "Animals and Man: A State of Blessedness"
(Light and Life Publishing, Minneapolis, USA)